A HARD THING
on a
BEAUTIFUL DAY

and other essays

ted kluck

GUT CHECK PRESS
Lansing, Michigan • Jackson, Tennessee

Published by Gut Check Press,
P.O. Box 10003
Lansing, Michigan 48901
www.gutcheckpress.com

Published in association with KD Enterprises.

Library of Congress Cataloging-in-Publication Data
Kluck, Ted
  A hard thing on a beautiful day / Ted Kluck.
      p. cm
  ISBN 978-1-7337954-0-1 (pbk.)
  ISBN 978-1-7337954-1-8 (audio bk)

  1. American Essays I. Title.

Library of Congress Control Number: 2019905932

CONTENTS

II. Pop Culture

III. Sports

IV. Gut Check

INTRODUCTION

Old Man Stuff: On Writing and Friendship

In the posh lobby of a New York City hotel, I once had a guy tell me that writing a book was "the hardest thing" he'd ever done. This particular guy had amazing abs, was always taking his shirt off, and was handsome in an almost unreal, Sears-catalog sort of way. Now, as a nice, Midwestern guy, my impulse was to just agree with him so that I could sort of "join" him in that moment. But I didn't, because it isn't. I've done all kinds of things that are way harder than writing books.

This—the *writing is super hard* thing—is also a thing that grim, joyless types will say from the stage at mostly-useless writing conferences. This is the kind of thing that my friend Zach Bartels and I will routinely make fun of at writing conferences. Because the thing is, writing is fun, not hard. And I think this is the case for most good writers. I started doing it because I wanted to do something fun—not because I wanted to "change the world" or "make people think."

I didn't know I liked writing. Growing up as a football player in a very blue-collar town in the Midwest in the '90s, there was really no category for a football player (big neck, buzz-cut, heavy-metal-in-Walkman, intimidating sneer) who also liked to write. I knew I loved reading and I knew I loved stories, but it took an injury, an operation, an incredibly sweet professor, and an even sweeter young lady (a little '90s theatre hottie who I met in college and then married) to convince me that writing vocationally was worth doing.

I've spent the rest of my life writing vocationally, which has given me the chance to live out the cliché that we often lay on young people when we say, "Find something you love to do and then do that for the rest of your life." Of course, getting married to writing-as-vocation is not unlike a real marriage in that there are fights, disappointments, and moments of despair interspersed with some really high and joyful highs. But much like loving KK—who appears in a lot of these essays—writing has pretty much come easy.

It was because of writing that I met Zach Bartels, whose idea this book was, and who is also a writer. He sat on the front row at a book signing I gave, and asked questions, and I could tell he was the kind of funny, irreverent, doesn't-take-himself-too-seriously guy that I could have serious fun with. I knew he was the kind of guy I could one day start a media empire with, and by "media empire" I mean the kind of company that could one day make us upwards of 2.5 *thousand* dollars a year. I know, heady stuff. But don't be intimidated by us—we're just regular guys.

After the signing, Zach asked me out. We went to lunch that weekend, at which time he smashed the door-panel of my car with his own car door. We've been together ever since—smoking cigars, recording podcasts, starting a company, laughing, laying on the cold concrete floor of a Bay City Park District bathroom after smoking too many cigars on a hot day, laughing, antiquing, watching movies, watching our kids grow up, renting movies at video stores, dining out like gentlemen, laughing, leaving some of the bullets from Zach's gun in the booth of a

Grand Ledge eatery, driving back for said bullets, and writing. We wrote the industry's seminal tome on Christian smoking (*The Christian Gentleman's Smoking Companion*) and wrote the Great American Novel together (*Re: Raptured*). Among other things.

But if you take away all the books, all the podcasts, all the money, and all the adulation we've received, Zach has performed a critical function in my life, and I mean this with zero percent irony: he has made writing fun. At times I have needed actual, direct convincing that writing is fun and that I shouldn't quit, and he has provided that. But mostly it has come indirectly, in that every single writing or media project we have done together has been deeply and manifestly *fun*. Every project has been the funnest version of what a project like that can be. In Christianity, we call this "joy."

When we met we were both young guys, in our twenties, who drew lots of energy from being at odds with our industry. Now we are middle-aged men, and one day, Lord-willing, we will be old men together, handing off the keys to a 2.5 thousand dollar-a-year industry to our sons. Again, heady stuff.

This book was Zach's idea and, short of writing the actual essays themselves, he has done the lion's share of the hard work on this—editing, cover design (most beautiful cover of my career; that's my son Maxim on it), illustrations, and page layout. So this book is, in addition to being for Maxim, for Zach. My friend.

Here's hoping it makes us 2.5 thousand dollars, which we can then use to purchase a skyscraper.

May, 2019

SPECIAL THANKS TO
OUR WHITE KNIGHTS

Eilidh Wilkinson

Samuel Barber

Daichi Tsuruta

Michael Stiles

Brad "B-Atch" Atchison

Andrew Raffa

…and all the Kickstarters.

PART I: LIFE

The Fire May be Dying and That's Okay

Originally Published in *The Jackson Sun*

The toe is a problem. The toe is purple and disfigured, thanks to the stomping it received by another large man wearing cleats. The toe can't bear any weight, meaning that for the next month and a half I can't squat, can't dead-lift, can't run, can't coach football the way I want to coach it (meaning immersively and with lots of physical involvement), can no longer be "different" (I'm an Enneagram 4 so this is important), and can't be fully "me."

Driving home through rural Illinois in the middle of the night, after my second annual leather helmet vintage football experience (with a broken toe) provided the right venue for existential thoughts. Leather helmet vintage football is the brainchild of an NFL historian name Simon Herrera and is a wonderful thing. And thanks to the semi-ethical fudging of some paperwork, it's a thing that allows me to suit up on a football field with my high-school-aged son which is, itself, the realization of a dream.

Last year I consciously looked out for him on the field, protected him, and made sure he was okay. This year, I realized, the tables had turned and he was doing the same for me, in that football *exists* for guys like him—guys who are young, fast, strong, and full of The Fire. This realization was both exceedingly sweet, and exceedingly sad. Gosh I love that kid.

The Fire is something I've had since roughly age 6 and could be described as a burning and almost constant desire to achieve, win, be unique, and be recognized for my

4 · A Hard Thing on a Beautiful Day

uniqueness. It has been, at times, inspirational and the beginning of some moderate achievements, and at other times has been aggravating and the thing keeping me from a good and biblical concept known as "contentment."

The Fire has caused me to go to the gym, lift heavy weights, read difficult books, write difficult books, and risk rejection in a variety of contexts both football and writing-related. It has—directly and indirectly—provided for my family. I'm thankful for it. It has also resulted in a broken leg, broken collarbone, broken thumb, broken finger, unmet expectations of many kinds, and now, a broken toe. I'm thankful that none of those injuries were worse, and am very aware that they could have been.

"If I'd just stayed home and watched television like a normal person this weekend, this wouldn't have happened," I told my wife in the dark. My poor wife was trapped with me, my broken toe, and my glum bloviating. Make no mistake about it: this sucked for her. I hoped, for her sake, she could at least get a Chipotle stop out of the trip.

"If you'd done that, you wouldn't be you," she said.

She was right.

I've been dabbling in contentment this year and, like all good things, the subtle shift has come directly from the Lord himself, and not from anything specific I've done to bring it about. I've tried, in a general sense, to cultivate the kinds of spiritual disciplines that bring about joy and contentment—like Bible reading, prayer, and membership at an amazing church where the Gospel is celebrated—but until now I've found it (contentment) hard to come by.

Each fall I've had the gnawing ache to compete in football. And each fall, losing those opportunities has devastated me in a way it shouldn't devastate a normal middle-aged man.

This year is different somehow. This year, the aches for football and even the aches to create and write something new, have been fewer and further between.

On the glum, dark drive home I realized how thankful I am to be getting help from people who love me. My wife speaking kind and true words, my son even taking a long pull behind the wheel. "Dad, the Lord gives and takes away," my son said, about my broken toe and my shortened game. He's right. At this age he's just parroting the things he's heard us say, and I hope that one day he internalizes them, but he's still right. Truth is truth.

It occurred to me that while it's fun, in a fleeting way, to be the high-achieving Alpha Dog with The Fire and all the ideas it brings, it's even better to be taken care of by the people who love me most.

Deconstructing Male Chitchat

I've recently been placed in situations where I've had to make what is referred to as "small talk" with a variety of men who I was meeting for the first time. These events, of course, primarily reveal my own insecurities and unrealistic expectations vis-à-vis the way certain events and interactions are "supposed" to go. They also make me really appreciate my actual male friends who are, without fail, really cool and honest and interesting.

In one such situation, a friend and I were brought in, ostensibly, as somewhat "honored" guests, in that we wrote a book about the thing that everybody was gathered for . . . except that nobody talked to us about that particular thing, almost nobody bought the book, and really nobody (besides a couple of genuinely friendly guys) made much of an effort to talk to us at all. That said, it gave me an opportunity to think about and archive the various types of male chitchat.

Stuff I've Bought Recently

"Yeah, I recently picked up the [brand name] [name of thing]. It shipped [really fast or really slow] . . . it's made out of pure [whatever it's made out of]. And the way you use it is to . . . [explains how it works]."

This is the point at which I stare off into space, at a spot just over the guy's left shoulder, so that he thinks I'm making eye contact but inside I'm really thinking, "I wish there was a social category that includes standing up and walking away from somebody when they're right in the middle of saying something, without looking like a jerk."

How Much Stuff Costs (See Above)

"It was really cheap."

Maybe this one is unique to West Michigan/The Upper Midwest, but it's a point of pride to sort of hitch up one's trousers and talk about the great deal you just got which, in other parts of the country, may seem a little classless.

Home Improvements I've Recently Made

Categories here include: lawn, garden, fencing, landscaping, siding, roofing, a fire pit, a new deck. The thought here is that your new (whatever) is really exciting to you, but the reality is, a point-by-point exposition on the new trim around the planters that run along the bottom part of your deck isn't going to be all that interesting to the other guy.

If I start looking at my phone it's not because I have a call, text, or email; it's because I am really, really bored. Also because I'm annoyed that my deck doesn't look as sweet as yours does.

My Job

This one is tricky because I'm usually genuinely curious about what people do for a living, so I kind of enjoy this one in certain contexts. What's really hard, though, is being on the outskirts of one of these talks, watching two men who are meeting each other for the first time have the "What do you do?" conversation. Awkwardness ensues, because invariably both men use the opportunity to size each other up, professionally, which is what that conversation is all about. Every once in a while a guy throws a curveball in response to the "What do you do?" question . . . something like, "As little as possible!" Which elicits an awkward chuckle from the other guy because it means that a.) the guy is unemployed or b.) the guy is so wealthy because of all his Business Conquests that he's semi-retired even though he doesn't look all that old.

In the case of b.), he "wins" the "What do you do?" conversation, which is why he loves having it so much and is the reason for the practiced and intentionally casual-sounding "As little as possible!" response.

Navigating this genre of chitchat is tough because if you make a lot of money but hate your job, you have to emphasize the money as it is your way to "win" the conversation, whereas if you have a really cool but financially unstable career you have to emphasize the coolness/freedom because that is your way of "winning."

If you think it's sad that guys think in categories like having a "winner" or "loser" in a conversation, you're absolutely right. It is sad. You're also probably a woman.

My Hot Wife

I think Promise Keepers made it a "thing" to talk about how hot/great your wife is, and how awesome you think she is, in the company of other men. They also made it a "thing" to turn that thing into a bumper sticker, which may even be more awkward than the conversation about the hot wife which is, in theory (thinking your wife is hot, talking about it), a really good thing, but in reality is actually kind of awkward for everybody who is involved.

It's primarily awkward because I don't know how to respond, because it's not socially appropriate to agree super-enthusiastically ("Yeah, your wife *is* really hot!") but it seems kind of rude to say nothing. The awkwardness increases like twenty-fold if the cell phone pictures come out during the conversation.

My Kids

Conversationally safe but usually boring, such that by the end I'd usually rather be talking *to* the other guy's kid than the other guy himself.

My Sports Interests

Conversationally safe but sometimes boring, depending on the sport and the people doing the talking.

My Outfit, Which Was Obviously (and Sadly) Constructed in Such a Way As To Make Me Look "Casual"

This isn't so much a type of chat as it is a look.

Conclusion

The thing about these "men gathering" situations is that they're usually motivated by some probably-church-related guilt about how men are "disconnected" and "need community" except that in most cases the men look miserable and like they'd rather be almost anywhere else doing almost anything else (usually alone). It occurs to me that it's nearly impossible to construct or contrive these situations, and that while most men genuinely want to talk, it's impossible to throw a bunch of them in a room and just say, "Here; talk!"

There are no easy answers to the Male Chitchat problem. I'm sure that there are things I do conversationally that bore and annoy people, so far be it from me to cast the first stone. I know, for example, that I have a tendency to nervous talk through silences, and also nervously begin asking a bunch of questions such that I take on a Larry-King-type-role in which I'm basically interviewing the other guy. I have no doubt that this is annoying, but I can't stop. And I also have no doubt that it's a hedge against having someone else ask *me* questions that I don't want to answer.

My friend pointed out that for a lot of men at a certain age they clamp off and kill that thing inside them that makes them interesting or weird or vital, such that what's left afterward is just a pair of khakis and a golf shirt. My exhortation would be to not clamp off and kill that thing. I'd much rather talk about your dream career as a kid or the skateboarder you thought was cool in the '90s, or the movie that you feel guilty about liking. All of those reveal more about you and are more interesting than your new grill. And also, I promise to not feel threatened by your career if you won't feel threatened by mine. That way, we can either move on to talking about the interesting parts of our jobs or, even better, not talk about our jobs at all.

I'm Proud of My Wife

Originally Published in *The Jackson Sun*

A week or so ago we finally watched *La La Land*, which is a twenty-minute movie (minus the musical numbers) about two creative people whose relationship doesn't work because they are both committed to their creative endeavors. Kristin and I have been married twenty years, all of which have been spent, at some level, trying to balance both of our creative endeavors.

On October 17th former President of the United States, George W. Bush, will be in Jackson for Union University's annual scholarship dinner. My wife, Kristin, who bakes the amazing muffins and scones that are enjoyed at the coffee shops on Union's campus, was selected to help make dessert for the President. It seems like a small thing, maybe, but my heart is full of pride and thankfulness for her.

Kristin and I, together, are perhaps the least-political couple ever. Part of this is a function of many years of self-employment—me as a writer and Kristin as a chef. When you're mired in the month-to-month, day-to-day, minute-to-minute grind of trying to pay bills and getting screwed over on health insurance each year (as is the lot in life of the self-employed person), you wake up one morning and realize you forgot to care about politics for like a decade.

But we both grew up in an era where there was still deep respect for the office of the POTUS. In grade school, letters were written to Ronald Reagan, and even if there was political disagreement, there was respect for the person and the office. Needless to say, this is no longer a thing.

My wife has been through a lot—and much of it has been my fault. When we met, she was the outstanding college student who loved reading and learning . . . while I loved bench pressing and tackling, until I got hurt, at which point I loved watching '90s movies and being depressed.

She got me through this period, by introducing me to writing. We cried together on the steps of our grim little house when I got my first book deal. We dreamed together about book deals (which came), movie deals (which have been a long time coming—but may be close), and all of the adventures we'd have (we've had many). But we've also had sin, troubles both financial and personal, and lots of hard repentance and reconciliation. I'm reminded of Psalm 66:10-12, which reads:

> For you, God, tested us;
>   you refined us like silver.
> You brought us into prison
>   and laid burdens on our backs.
> You let people ride over our heads;
>   we went through fire and water,
>   but you brought us to a place of abundance.

Jackson is our place of abundance because it represents perhaps the first time we've really been able to be creative *together*. Kristin is flourishing as a chef, and it just reminds me of all the sacrifices she made—for me—to get us here.

I won't get to see President Bush enjoying her desserts,

because it costs like $20,000 to get into that room. But I know how he'll feel because I've enjoyed them myself—in dingy apartments, overseas, in good times and in bad, in sickness and in health, 'til death do us part. I hope he enjoys them. I thank God for the hands that made them.

The Blogosphere Killed Bin Laden

I turned on my computer the other day and found out from Facebook that Osama Bin Laden was dead. And before I had a chance to really even react, or feel an emotion even remotely akin to "genuine" or "my own," the self-same Facebook that delivered the news also delivered links to a bunch of blogs telling me the "right" way to feel about it. Like (for example) I was allowed to be a little happy because we'd finally hunted down and killed an enemy but not *too* happy because even the heavily-bearded, verminish-looking Bin Laden was created in God's image, and so on and so forth.

The result was that if my range of feelings vis-à-vis Bin Laden could be boiled down to one word, it would be this: nothing.

Because in the span of about ten minutes I found out about Bin Laden and then had at my fingertips the means through which to be told *how* I should feel, think, and talk about Bin Laden, which essentially rendered the whole Bin Laden *experience* (if you will) something less than my own. It's a crass comparison to make but it was kind of like reading a whole bunch of movie reviews telling me how I should feel about a certain movie to the extent that I no longer wanted to see the movie, one way or the other. I, essentially, skipped the Bin Laden movie.

The truth of the matter is this: I kind of feel a little bit bummed that I missed out on the experience of being excited that we killed Bin Laden. I feel like pre-social media this would have been a more interesting deal altogether. Which raises the question (and I'm not asking facetiously this time, I'm, like, really asking): Was it better back then? Better, in the sense that we really experienced these things together in a more tangible way. For example, I remember where I was when the Gulf War started (the gym, in my hometown, with everybody sort of huddled around the TV there). I remember where I was when OJ Simpson had his famous car chase (at college orientation, with everybody, again, huddled, and kind of experiencing/reacting together).

And here's an even more awkward/potentially-terrible question: Was it better when we had to wait until Sunday to get the final word on this stuff? The blogosphere has kind of rendered every day Sunday to the degree that if we have even an inkling of curiosity we can find a post or archived sermon that addresses the Royal Wedding, Rob Bell, Bin Laden, or the NFL Draft. In a way this is a tremendous blessing but in a way it kind of takes a little bit of the starch out of Sunday. And in a way it has maybe taken a little bit of the starch out of *your* pastor because somebody else's pastor probably said it better and more eloquently, online, on Tuesday.

In true postmodern fashion I have no answers here, just a bunch of questions, sent out into the void.

On Selling a House

Like many Americans this summer, we are trying to sell a home. This is a pride-swallowing siege that involves living in your house while at the same time basically making it look like nobody has ever lived there before. Our house looks like a magazine house now.

Aside: Our house is a charming three-bedroom, 2.5 bath with an office and a huge basement built about 8 years ago (by us) in Grand Ledge, MI. There's also a neighborhood pool and fitness center. If you enjoy reading my books and want to *live in my* house, drop me a line. This house has hosted many lavish Gut Check Press parties, is home to the boxing ring where I once managed and sparred with a pro fighter, and is home to "Studio A" and "Studio B" where we record The Gut Check Podcast. (If you want, I can leave the boxing ring in the basement for you.)

Interesting and soul-sucking bits of feedback gleaned from our realtor after she showed the house, after we had spent like 48 hours doing nothing but cleaning it:

1. "There was a toilet brush present." Which, apparently, implies that actual people live in the home and use the toilets. I will, in the future, be hiding my toilet brushes in the trunk of my car during showings which sounds like the saddest thing in the world because it *is* the saddest thing in the world because it implies that I am a grown man hiding a toilet brush in the trunk of his car.

2. "You'll need to clear everything off the kitchen counters." And this includes the KitchenAid mixer which weighs roughly 400 pounds, and also everything else that you would ever use in the process of preparing and eating food, making it, again, really inconvenient to live in the house right now.

3. "This office is 10 × 10 . . . it doesn't look like 10 × 10." To which I replied, " . . . "

4. "One buyer was concerned about crumbs on the kitchen counter." This is definitely a deal-breaker. I am committed, for as long as the house is on the market, to never even enter my kitchen again and also to never let my two small boys anywhere near it, which is, of course, totally feasible. It's disconcerting to realize that part of selling a house involves allowing total strangers—who are apparently also very rude—walk through your home and make judgments about, not only the home, but also you. In no other aspect of life would this happen. That's how desperate we are to sell a house.

I've long thought, watching my share of *House Hunters International*, that buying a home brings out the absolute worst and most shallow aspects of the human heart. We would find ourselves saying, "Do they only put despicable people on this show?" When in fact, the people are probably well within the realm of normal, but it's the process of buying a home that actually turns someone into a raving, irrational, lunatic because the process of buying a home gives people the illusion that they can have a little slice of perfection in an imperfect world. And naturally, when they don't get absolute perfection, they completely lose all sense of perspective.

I've come away from this process feeling more burdened for our realtor in part because she probably sees more human-heart-related darkness and selfishness on a given day than almost anyone . . . and she's getting it from both sides, meaning, she's getting a steady dose of ridiculous irrationality from the buyers, and also a steady dose of thin-skinned anger and impatience from me. This must really suck for her.

I'm reminded, in this process, that God must increase while I must decrease. I feel like I'm decreasing a little more every day.

A Hard Thing on a Beautiful Day

Originally Published in *The Jackson Sun*

When my son, Maxim, was three years old, we adopted him from an orphanage just outside of Kiev, Ukraine.

When we met him he was so weak that he couldn't even walk up or down the stairs by himself and would, literally, blow over in a stiff breeze. It was sad and hard and we cried a lot while we tried to feed him and build him back up.

Yesterday he competed in the Tennessee State Cross Country Championships in Knoxville on an idyllic day in an idyllic park in a scenario in which he was lined up with knees bent, with an eye-of-the-tiger look on his face, surrounded by three hundred wildly-pubescent junior high boys. He's in sixth grade, running against mostly eighth-graders. He qualified for this by finishing in the Top 25 at the state qualifying meet in Memphis last weekend. He has run through mud, slop, and rain, and has run so hard that he's puked after races.

But a funny thing happened before his race. Before his race, the middle school girls raced and while they were racing I cried. I was overcome by emotion watching courageous kids do a hard thing on a beautiful day. I was moved by the kids themselves, the mountains in the background, and their families. Some of the girls cried after their race, because they were in so much pain. I tried to blend in with the crowd, in terms of my own crying, because I felt sheepish about it.

Here's why I got emotional: so many things about

adult life are so miserable (and by this I mean politics and social media and the way people act on Twitter and the way that all situations are almost hopelessly complicated). And by contrast, kids running a race in a really hard and non-malicious way had a cleansing effect on my soul. It, quite literally, made me feel better. I am thankful for it.

What's more, I responded to this competitive environment in ways that I don't, normally. Normally, competition turns me into the most horrible version of myself. I become a dog. I want to win and everyone else to be crushed. I didn't feel this way yesterday, at all. I was really happy for Maxim and really happy for all the other kids, too. Happy for their sacrifices, and happy for their efforts. I clapped for kids I didn't know, and would never meet. I felt better.

When Maxim crossed the finish line—which was big and official and professional-looking—I ran back to where he was doubled-over, gasping for air, and I held him and cried on him. I cried because I remembered his orphanage, where they never let him outside and barely turned on the lights. I remembered all our afternoons, sprinting together on the soccer field at West Jackson. I remembered feeding him when he was three and frail and couldn't get enough. I remembered how much he likes quoting our favorite movies like *Tommy Boy* and *Moneyball* and how good he is at delivering the right lines at the right times.

I looked at my son and my wife and the sun and thought that God has been too kind to me.

I felt better.

On Purchasing Life Insurance

My wife used to answer phones for a life insurance company on the gazillionth floor of a tall building in Indianapolis. I was in college. We were both so young, I think we just thought it was cool that we got to ride an elevator and could see that much of the city from her window, but neither of us had much of an idea of what went on there. What goes on there is this: a much more complicated version of Fantasy Football in which instead of projecting touchdowns the company crunches numbers to predict how long I'm going to live. It could be called "Fantasy Life Expectancy."

A decade ago I bought a term life policy that is about to run out, and am currently running the gauntlet of a new life insurance purchase so that the people I love can have some money when I die which may be the single most depressing thing in the world to think about.

> **Agent:** "Have you ever had a life expectancy workup done?"
>
> **Me:** "What is that?"
>
> **Agent:** "This battery of tests that determines how long you'll probably live."
>
> **Me:** "That sounds awful. People do this?"
>
> **Agent:** "So that's a 'no?'"

I have received roughly thirty emails from this woman (who for the record is a very good insurance agent) in the last three days, all covering such topics as exactly how many cigars I smoke in a given month, my "net worth," and any noteworthy changes in my weight. File all of this in a folder entitled, "As If Being In Your Late Thirties and Feeling Those Particular Mortality and Achievement-Related Feelings Wasn't Enough; Now There's This." David Foster Wallace wrote an 800-page meta-joke on boredom and apathy entitled *The Pale King*, and it seems appropriate here. Maybe I'll re-read it.

"What you need to do before the blood test is just drink lots of water and, like, go on a diet," she explains. "To make sure your sodium and everything is low."

Me: "Where will this test take place?"

Agent: "They come to your house."

Me: "That sounds weird . . . and by weird I mean somehow, medically, below-board."

Agent: " . . . "

After which I signed like 55 pieces of paper authorizing the Life Insurance Company to assess how likely it is that I'll die before they recoup a lot of money from me.

Agent: "Skydiving?"

Me: "No."

She then produced a binder full of papers which, in great detail, define what constitutes a "smoker." The fact that some poor copywriter had to produce that makes me so sad that I think I've lost a year or two of my life just thinking about it. I refrain from making this quip to her.

Before the end of the meeting I just wanted an acknowledgment, from her, that all of what we were discussing and signing is unspeakably weird. I mean, I realize the semi-necessity of all of it, and even realize the necessity of endless reams of paper devoted to backside-covering fraud-reducing measures, etc. I get that. Being an adult is, at some level, almost all about that, which is why people get all wistful and longy when they write about *quote-unquote* simpler times. And I understand that people need jobs, and that being a good life insurance agent is a noble calling. I just want her to acknowledge the weirdness.

"It's just so weird, what we're talking about," I say, making eye contact and even semi-cocking an eyebrow. She's my mom's age and has, no doubt, seen it all. She seems completely immune to whatever depressed, not-devilish charm I'm conjuring. I'm really pushing now. I want to close the cosmic, existential deal I've made in my own head, with her (unbeknownst, of course, to the actual her). I wait a second for her to respond.

"Well, yeah . . . I mean . . . yeah." She says.

And I leave satisfied.

People at My Old College Are Losing Their Minds

Originally Published in *The Jackson Sun*

Taylor University is my old college, not my alma mater, because I didn't graduate from there. I actually graduated from IUPUI, which is known in some circles as the Harvard of the near-west side of Indianapolis. I was at Taylor for two and a half years. Five semesters. It was good. Notice I said that it was neither "Amazing" nor "The Worst." It wasn't the most incredibly formative 2.5 years of my life, but it was far from the hardest. I met my wife and my non-spousal best friend while I was there.

Taylor students, faculty, and alums are freaking out because Vice President Mike Pence was booked to speak at graduation. This is, apparently, The Worst. I know this because of petitions, social media, strongly-worded e-mails, and think pieces—which are all the 2019 versions of "talking." The sky is falling over Upland, Indiana, which is a very tiny town in America's Heartland and is also where Taylor is. Also, I say "America's Heartland" with zero-percent snark, because I'm from there and it's still hard to not get romantic about it.

Now, to be clear, nobody is losing their mind to anybody's face, because in the Midwest (and also the South), pleasantness trumps all.

Here's the crux of the issue, as I see it: Taylor is an Evangelical Christian school where parents and donors are probably mostly conservative, but professors and students are mostly liberal because it's a college in 2019 and

Trump is the President, and as such you're not really allowed to say you're a conservative for coolness and rep-protecting (and maybe actual convictional) reasons. Outrage ensues. The national media loves nothing more than outrage and divisiveness and Christians falling on their collective faces, and has covered the outrage accordingly.

I think everyone at Taylor has forgotten that the graduation address is the most meaningless twenty minutes in American public life. It's the most vapid, easily-ignored content, delivered (usually) in a gym or on a football field that manages to be hot, moist, and incredibly uncomfortable. No offense to Mike Pence, but he won't say anything at Taylor that anyone will really remember, because the day isn't about Mike Pence but is rather very much about each individual graduate. The angriest moment in the Mike-Pence-at-Taylor-experience, is *this moment*.

When I was at Taylor in the mid-'90s you were allowed to be a Republican or a Democrat or a mostly-oblivious meathead (spoilers: this is what I was), but part of how you looked cool in the mid-'90s was by not caring (thank goodness!). In 2019 you are not allowed to *not* be super outraged, one way or another. This is disconcerting, for Taylor, and also for everywhere.

We Midwesterners used to be pretty good at dealing with disappointment. We would get a bit of bad news—be it at work, or from a news story—go home, vent a little, and then get back in our trucks or on our tractors and just kind of . . . deal with it. Dealing with it used to be our greatest strength. Perhaps the Taylor community can reclaim a bit of this spirit and just . . . deal with it.

Lawn Stuff and Minimalism: A Confession
Originally Published in *The Jackson Sun*

I have a very deep and real understanding that there are important things going on in the world. Some of those important things include school shootings, the #MeToo movement, and the Royal Wedding. Two of these are worthy of any normal human being's time and attention. Personally, I spend an inordinate amount of time thinking about my lawn. Not, however, about its lushness or green-ness or making it more awesome because those are the kinds of lawn-related thoughts that bring a man pleasure. I think about my lawn in the context of lawns that belong to the other men (mostly older than me) in my neighborhood. I think about the fact that I care for my own lawn while most of them hire out their lawncare. I think of them judging my lawn (and by extension, me) with their eyes as they drive by and wave amicably. I read things into their amicable waves—things that are (probably) dumb and just figments of my writerly imagination.

If I mow my lawn on a Saturday or Sunday, it is usually Tuesday or Wednesday when I experience my first pang of worry that it needs to be mowed again. When I take idyllic evening constitutionals with my wife of 21 years in the dusk hours, my mind usually isn't filled with peace, tranquility, and thankfulness; rather, it is filled with envious thoughts of my neighbors' lawns. I can usually hear a weed whip somewhere in the distance and then say some romantic words to my wife, along the lines of, "I really need to edge our lawn."

She is, as they say, living the dream.

On any given rainless day in my neighborhood a variety of pickup trucks can be seen rumbling by, towing the sorts of trailers that are really just metal frames and slats of wood and atop which sit lawncare implements of various kinds—lawn tractors, push-mowers, edgers. I see this as the ultimate in conspicuous consumption. The equivalent of a red Corvette convertible. A real "look at me"-type deal.

I would like to see it as a badge of honor that I care for my own lawn, but that would imply that it brings me some sort of smug pleasure, which it doesn't. It just feels dumb to pay for something I can totally do myself.

Speaking of smug pleasure (which is absolutely the best kind): Last night we watched the Netflix documentary, *Minimalism*. It can be summarized thusly: a handful of young guys doing what young guys do really well, which is bloviating about how getting rid of a bunch of their stuff made them happier. I loved it. It made me miss being a young guy who would bloviate about similar things. It was the kind of documentary that made you feel smarter for having watched it, though I couldn't pinpoint exactly how or why. It was the kind of thing that there will be dozens more of on Netflix in another six months, thereby making it an ironic parody of itself. But it isn't there yet.

Nor is my unredeemable lawn obsession—which, like the stuff in the minimalism doc—is really something that I need to just emotionally unburden myself of. Like Instagram, it is a dumb way to compete. It is also a very real possibility that nobody in my neighborhood has even thought of my lawn at all until, ironically, their daily paper flies over their perfectly-edged sidewalk and hits their doorstep with a satisfying, Rockwellian thud, and they see this column.

If Rockwell were to paint my place, he would paint a cool-looking mid-century house that is in need of a good paint job. He would paint whatever it looks like for a dad to play catch with his kids while at the same time fighting the temptation to check email on his phone. He would paint a lawn that tries hard, looks decent about 70% of the time, but hasn't quite arrived yet. In that, it is not unlike its owner.

Vulnerability as Leverage
(And Other Potentially Hideous Things)

My wife works in an office. It is, by and large, a great office filled with great people who are, for the most part, kind and gracious and affirming. Being that she works in an office, though, she occasionally has meetings where they show TED Talks which is a phenomenon that has totally escaped me being that I am a.) self-employed and b.) not on social media. Sometimes she comes home and shows me the talks if they're in any way thought provoking.

Today's talk was by a very polished former academic named Brene' Brown who had that "I just crawled out of the hole of academia and peer-reviewed journals and am totally lapping up the real attention I'm getting from real people in a real audience" look about her. She was a really good speaker and storyteller. Her thesis was that quote/unquote *vulnerability* is kind of the key to everything if we define everything as love, joy, creativity, and feeling "worthy." She didn't really define vulnerability which, in my opinion, would have been the more important thing to try to define. Her point, though, was that people who feel "worthy" (i.e., valued, i.e., creative, i.e., successful) are always "vulnerable" people, but not in the sense of small-child-walking-alone-in-the-dark vulnerability, but rather being-honest-with-you-conversationally vulnerability.

Caveat: For Christians vulnerability has a completely different set of definitions and activities that go along with it—like repentance, trusting in a God we can't see, surrendering to that God, and then being accountable to others.

These are the things that, for us, comprise vulnerability. But that wasn't what she was talking about at all.

What was weird about the TED Talk context for a vulnerability speech is that at the very moment that vulnerability becomes a tactic or a technique or a sales tool, by definition (mine or hers) it ceases to be actual vulnerability and probably toes the very fine line of manipulation. Basically what I'm saying is that if I am aware that I'm being vulnerable in order to get you to open up or like me or feel comfortable with me or buy my book or give me a five-star review or love my TED talk then I am probably, at some level, screwing with you. Even if I'm not entirely aware that I'm doing it. This is the total-depravity part of the equation which is, by the way, the part of Calvinism that makes the most sense to me.

This is why I need Christ

Our Guy Pulls Weeds. Yours?

Originally Published in *The Jackson Sun*

Earlier today at work—I'm a professor at Union University—I had an idyllic college-professor moment in that I was sitting in an unspeakably hipster coffee shop working with a student on a writing project. If I were a better-looking college professor, it would have been prime admissions-brochure fodder.

I'm still in a bit of a "honeymoon" phase in year three of my job, in which I still occasionally say things like, "I get paid to talk about books; this is amazing!" However, I am also adult enough to see and realize that no place is perfect, as is no person. I know that there are political squabbles on campus, and my response to those squabbles is usually just to bury my head in the sand and pretend they don't exist. My old-school dad once told me, "Keep your head down and keep your mouth shut and just do your job." I think I was eight at the time (he was really old school), but I've pretty much adopted that as a lifelong work policy.

All of that said, I saw something today at the coffee shop that I want to share with the world—not because I'm trying to leverage it in any sort of coy, cunning way[1].

Here's what I saw: Union University President, Dub

---

[1] I think in nearly twenty years in the workforce I've shown a stunning inability to ever really be able to leverage anything. Ask my wife, who keeps our books, how bad I am at leveraging.

Oliver, in his usual slacks and bowtie, walking alone across campus and pausing to bend down, pull a clump of weeds, and then slink over to a trashcan to throw them away. For a while, in the distance, I didn't know it was a clump of weeds, and thought it might have been a sheaf of papers or something presidential that he had dropped.

It was for sure weeds.

When he entered the unspeakably hipster coffee shop, I gave him a bro-hug[2] and asked if he was pulling weeds. He sheepishly replied that he was, and then I sheepishly explained that I wouldn't tell anybody about it. We laughed. And then I sat down to write this column. Writers are liars.

Far be it from me to attach tons of meaning and significance to a president pulling weeds on his campus. But because I'm not the other kind of columnist (the kind that writes about foreign policy and the economy and Trump), this is the kind of thing I am charmed by, and end up writing about.

Also, far be it from me to know a ton about Dub Oliver as a person or a college president. I know that he has been gracious and kind in his dealings with me, I always enjoy chatting with him, and I would totally send my kid to our school (and probably will).

But in the college business I sometimes feel like smugness and arrogance is our chief export. We're producing a generation of expert bloviators, but I wonder if we're producing the kinds of kids who care enough to bend

---

[2] In addition to his other fine qualities, Dub shows great patience when I occasionally act like a fratty idiot with everybody, in spite of the fact that I'm in no way young.

down and pick up a clump of weeds? It's about seeing something that needs to be done and just doing it. It's about caring about something in a personal way. I would be remiss to attach a bunch of morality to this event, or use it to draw a bunch of conclusions, other than to say that it was just *decent*. And I wonder if I, myself, have lost the ability to just do basic, decent things from time to time?

Today I felt pretty proud of our guy for doing an entirely decent and unglamorous thing, for being willing to (literally) get his hands dirty, and for caring about the appearance of our campus in the same way that I would probably care about the appearance of my home if I were to have Dub over for dinner. It's nice to see the person who talks the most about leadership, actually doing it.

Honoring a Fallen Friend

An hour ago I received a phone call informing me that the father of my best childhood friend had taken his life. I could tell from my own father's tone of voice that he had bad news. After receiving the call, I called my wife and wept. I wept for his family, for the secret pain that he was feeling, and for my own sins. I felt the full flush of my own humanity—my own aging and decaying body, my own sin-stained heart . . . and the unrelenting onslaught of sin and death in this dark world. I wept for the relative triviality of my own semi-public life—of checking how many people listen to my podcast, of my latest project on pro football. I wept that it will be late-afternoon before I can hug my kids and kiss my wife.

One of the problems with being a memoirist is that, to some degree, something hasn't fully "happened" for me until I've written about it. And the writing is, in this case, a hedge against sitting at my desk and weeping all afternoon. It's a means of understanding and dealing, and it is my weakness. I lack that inner wellspring of strength that some people have and I need others to help give it to me. I beg the forgiveness of my readers. Sometimes (often) what I write is for me—for my own pleasure, my own laughs, and to feed my own need for approval. Sometimes (like today) it's an attempt to use words to honor a lovely person and to try to understand something that is so completely *hard*.

My friend's dad had a preternatural gift for making people feel special and honored. Unlike many men in his generation he had absolutely no problem saying "Great job!" or "Congratulations!" When I was in his presence, I felt like John Riggins, like a Hall of Famer, instead of the wholly mediocre small-town athlete that I actually was. He was the insurance guy in town. I'm sure there were others, technically, but he was the only one that mattered. His office was a regular stop on our BMX-bike tour of Hartford City.

We would stop in and raid the ashtray in his office which was always filled with an assortment of Chicklets gum and butterscotch candy (which I'm sure was actually for clients but felt like it was refreshed each day for us). And if he ever had a problem with the fact that we routinely spray-painted end zones and base-paths in his backyard, or built slam-dunk ramps in his driveway, or used his satellite dish as a backstop . . . he never showed it. We watched Super Bowls together.

"Hey T!" he would shout from the driveway, whenever I would walk, drive, or jog by. This was always accompanied by a big, toothy smile. I will miss this deeply, as each time I visit my hometown, more of what I loved about it is gone. Buildings have fallen down. People have moved away or died. Another factory has closed. At some level the beauty and simplicity of childhood (of which he was a big part) has ruined me on the realities of adulthood. It is in these moments that I need Jesus the most.

When people I love die I am reminded, like Paul at the end of Romans 7, that I am wretched in my own *body of death*. It is in these moments that I need the hope of Romans 8—that there is now no condemnation for those who are in Christ Jesus, and that the law of the Spirit of

Life has set me free from the law of sin and death. I need that freedom both today and in eternity.

It breaks my heart that Mitch's dad battled sadness, pain, and hopelessness and it makes me sad that I didn't and couldn't help him. It reminds me that we often have no sense of the magnitude of the battles that people are fighting behind closed doors. I'm reminded that even for the habitually cheerful, there is a moment (or more) when life becomes unmanageable and when the heart grows faint.

From the end of the earth I call to you when my heart is faint. Lead me to the rock that is higher than I.

Psalm 61:2

Dear Inane Music at Restaurants: Please Stop

Originally Published in *The Jackson Sun*

My wife and I are frequenters of a particular local Mexican restaurant (which distinction, granted, narrows it to like 93 places). We were having dinner there the other night when we realized: "Wait, this is really nice and quiet and relaxing. What's missing?"

What was missing was, of course, the particular brand of inane, straight-down-the-fairway American Mexican restaurant playlist which amounts to a bunch of "I'm just relaxin' with my beer" songs by artists like Jimmy Buffett and others who (for inexplicable reasons) want to sound like Jimmy Buffett. Musically, this is the least-defensible of all genres. It makes "Bro Country" feel like Rachmaninoff. It's ear-splitting, not because of the loudness, but because of the stupidity it both celebrates and at the same time, fosters.

The music is such a part of the fabric of dining out in America that it is like the auditory pebble in one's shoe—aggravating, but if you can't stop and take it out, you learn to live with it. You talk a little louder. You block it out.

Often when I watch restaurant scenes in period-specific movies, I'll say something like, "That place looks awesome." What I'm realizing is that movie restaurants look awesome because there are zero televisions on the walls tuned to SportsCenter or a yacht race or music videos, and there are zero guys singing about just enjoying some beers with their buds. What movie directors realize (but the American restaurant industry has failed to) is that people don't go out to eat to listen to music or watch television.

Would the Italian restaurant scene where Michael kills Solozzo in *The Godfather* be improved if there was a guy in the background singing about *wastin' away again in Margaritaville*? How about the "I'll have what she's having" scene in *When Harry Met Sally*? Would that have been better if Billy Crystal had been staring slack-jawed over her shoulder at a re-run of ESPN's *Pardon the Interruption*?

Here's the thing: not every experience has to *deliver every experience*. One doesn't, generally, go out to a restaurant thinking, "I can't wait to get there and watch something amazing on television." Or, "I hope there's some incredible music playing while I'm eating my burrito." This ethic has, sadly, permeated other aspects of American life. Going to an NFL or NBA game in 2019 is an exercise in paying a lot of money to watch television in a bigger room where the food is more expensive and you have to pay for parking.

The thing is, every American has, in his or her pocket, a conduit to every single inane thing that anyone would ever want to watch or listen to or comment upon. This reality would, one would think, render restaurant music or screens, redundant.

But alas, the meal out is still an occasion to watch Kid Rock waggle his pelvis, and watch Tony Kornheiser scream at somebody on mute. Sometimes at the same time. Sometimes while also listening to a florid-faced moron sing an ode to his cold one.

All things being equal, I think I might just stay home.

When Christmas Fails

And by "failing" I don't mean the actual Christmas (i.e., the birth of Christ and all that that entails) . . . rather, I mean the cultural expectations associated with Christmas, which is that we're supposed to always feel happy, hopeful, relaxed, and fulfilled in every way but especially materially and relationally. Here are a few examples of people for whom Christmas is difficult.

1. **People Who Work Hard with Their Bodies.** The new Keurig you're getting for Christmas has been packaged, scanned, shipped, loaded, and unloaded by scores of people who get up early, work in the cold, and work long hours doing things you wouldn't want to do in conditions that you wouldn't want to do them in. They get yelled at, at work, and the logistics industry is no respecter of the following: Christmas traditions, family, travel, icy roads, feelings, or sleeping in. It *is* a respecter of this: making sure you get your PajamaGram on time.

I have a newfound respect for such people, because now I am one. I wrote the following to my wife in an email today, trying to explain what I experience every morning:

"But it *does* have a nightmarish quality. I wish you could see it. It's dark, it's cold, it's loud . . . people are sometimes mean. It's the very definition of gray, industrial, drab, and devoid of beauty. Now, there's something cool about surviving that each day . . . and there *is* a sense of accomplishment. But it is quantifiably hard and scary. There are so many potential mistakes to make . . . and so many ways to get hurt. It's like being in a movie I never thought I'd be in . . . which speaks to the next point: it's making me question my perception of who and what I actually am. Am I a promising writer/teacher or am I just a grunt? The answer is that right now I'm both, by necessity. But each day, it's harder to think of myself as anything but a grunt. What it takes out of me (by nature of the early hour, the physicality, etc.) makes it hard for me to feel like I can be the promising writer/teacher."

2. **People Whose Families Are, for Whatever Reason, a Mess.**

   This applies to more people than you might think. This being a fallen, sin-saturated world, our relationships (even with the people we love) can seem hopelessly fractured or, at the very least, less than perfect. Christmas magnifies this feeling, although theoretically, being reminded of the birth of our Savior should have the opposite effect.

3. **People Pleasers.**

   When you're a people pleaser, you derive a good bit of your self-worth from making sure the people around you are happy and fulfilled. Christmas magnifies this as well. You spend so much time meeting the emotional and relational needs of the people around you—refereeing conflicts, middle-manning other awkward relationships, making sure everyone's gifts are perfect—that you can end up quietly resenting every-

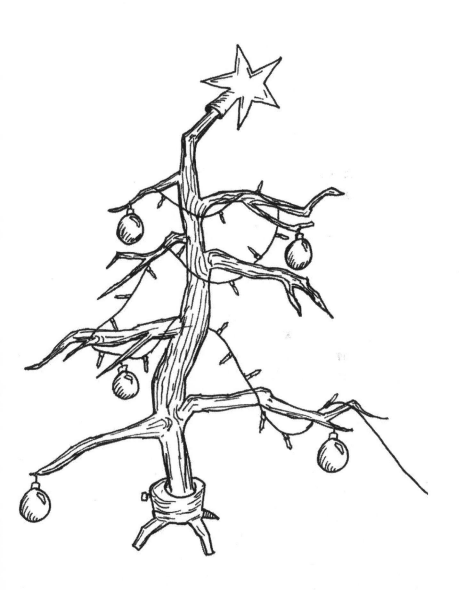

one (although you'd never tell them that, because it would hurt *their* feelings).

4. **People Who are Sick or Dying.**
A week or so ago, a friend found out that her father has Stage 4 pancreatic cancer. This cast Christmas in a different light for her . . . and for us as we wept with her. We're reminded of our mortal bodies, of our limitations, of our inability to engineer or purchase utopian lives for ourselves.

5. **People Who Don't Have "Something to Look Forward To."**

In writing, I hate "tacked on" Christian endings. I hate sometimes being cajoled, by editors, to do this. But I'm reminded that in the five scenarios above (and in all the others), my only hope is Christ. My hope isn't in getting enough sleep. It's not in everybody in my house getting along on Christmas Day, so that I can relax. It's not in the health or strength of my body, which will one day fail. It's not even in the prospect of restored relationships, some of which are fractured because of my own sins. It's not in "something to look forward to," like a trip, or a new piece of electronic gadgetry. My only hope, in any of this, is in a Savior who is sovereign and good, who has numbered my days (even Christmases) and who purchased me with His blood.

Getting to experience this (God's goodness) is the truth that allows winter depressives (like me) to continue getting up each morning.

An Open Letter to the Medina, TN Traffic Control Safety Program

Originally Published in *The Jackson Sun*

Dear Medina, TN, Traffic Control Safety Program,

When I was sixteen and learning to drive, my parents always told me, "Don't drive angry." Unfortunately my parents weren't writers, and couldn't similarly implore me to avoid "writing angry." (Subtext: I'm about to write angry.)

I returned home from work this afternoon to find a piece of correspondence from your office. It had that tell-tale "depressing civic office" look about it, and as I ripped into the envelope I knew in my heart what I would find: A traffic citation for driving 66 in a 55 MPH zone in a small edge of Medina which I drove through on my way to the kind of bucolic West Tennessee hamlet that doesn't resort to lowbrow, gauche, video-controlled traffic citations: Milan. Ahh, Milan (not pronounced like the one in Italy), city of dreams.

Anyway.

I take full responsibility as the kind of roguish charlatan who shakes his fist at authority by driving 66 in a 55. I own that. I am a flinty-eyed bad boy. If I smoked cigarettes I would roll them in the sleeves of my fitted white tee shirt. Thankfully no one was injured or put in danger by my devil-may-care actions.

Where was this hardened bad-boy going on his fabled rubber-burning jaunt through Medina? To the Milan High School library, which is where all the other flinty-eyed bad boys in the area hang out and plot similar acts of mayhem. And also to read works of young adult fiction.

To the good, law-abiding citizens of Medina: this isn't about you. You're just trying to get by and live happily in a community free from the kinds of societal scum who drive eleven over the posted speed limit. My fight isn't with you or your police department. It's with your video cameras and by that I mean the cameras themselves and not even the people who run them. It's complicated. So please—Medina citizen—don't glare at me in Tulum next Sunday when you have the luxury of knowing who I am (I'll be the flinty-eyed bad boy) and I don't have the same luxury. Again, I'm not mad at you or your town. It's the cameras.

And just to clear up any ambiguity: This bad boy will be writing a check in the amount of $50.00 to cover the violation. I will not be seeking my day in court—primarily because a day in court involves another white-knuckle drive through the video-monitored streets of Medina. That's not a drive I'm willing to make.

Has this experience caused me to do the sort of deep, dark-room, late-night, soul-searching self-evaluation that is part of every cop narrative (television or film) ever made? You bet it has. I will be watching *Heat* and *Goodfellas* and *American Gangster* tonight just to be able to once again take inventory of which characters I see myself in (spoiler: all of them).

Here's how I see this playing out: after my evening of soul-searching, I will unroll the cigarettes from my shirt-sleeve and dramatically flush them down the toilet. I will burn my aggressive-looking red jacket and replace it with something in a nice beige. And I will never again drive eleven miles per hour over the posted speed limit. I will have been changed—reformed—and the system will have *worked*.

Thank you, Medina, TN, Traffic Control Program. You have changed a life.

Sincerely,

Ted A. Kluck

I'm New Here: Reflections on Six Months in Jackson, TN

Originally Published in *The Jackson Sun*

When we visited Jackson to interview at Union University last spring it was hot and disorienting—not unlike running a low-grade fever. I immediately loved Union and my future colleagues, but as a lifelong Northerner, the South felt foreign and imposing. Six months later it occurs to me that Jackson, while a weird place to visit, may in fact be the perfect place to live.

That said, it's been an interesting adjustment, and I've learned a lot about life down here.

I've learned that church is not just a place to pray, sing hymns, and listen to a sermon; it can also look like a Bally's Total Fitness and be the place where your kid plays all of his baseball and basketball games.

I've learned that this conflating of church and public life can, on one level, be very healthy but on another very dangerous level render church just another rote, expected and non-transformative aspect of civic life.

I've learned that people down here don't use the word "conflating" and I love them for that.

I've learned what "bless your heart" actually means— which is something along the lines of "what you've just done is embarrassing for you and horribly disappointing for me."

I've learned the meaning of "meat and three," and enjoyed more delicious barbeque in the last six months than in all of my previous years, combined. I've dined in a local restaurant with centerpieces as large as a toddler.

I've learned that the Uniform of Male Respectability is a pair of khaki pants, a dark blue blazer, and a regimental bowtie. It's a look that says, "Trust me with your investment banking" or, "Send your kid to my university."

Sartorially, I've learned that there was a certain understatedness to the North that doesn't exist down here. A recent visit to a private school evening fundraiser revealed everything along a fashion spectrum from "I'll be feeding the chickens later" to "I'll be boarding a private jet to Vegas for my friend's bachelorette party."

I've learned that hipsters—for all their striving to be wholly unique—dress exactly the same everywhere.

At the self-same event I've learned what it feels like to try to explain to the kind photographer from *VIP Magazine* that I am not, in fact, a VIP and then have him, again kindly, convince me that I am. I've learned that the whole *VIP Magazine* negotiation made me feel actually good.

I've learned what a truly beautiful sunset looks like— as Carl Sandburg wrote, "like blood-red poppies, for a garden, to walk in."

I've learned what it feels like to see the sun between the months of November and March, and it feels really, really good.

I've enjoyed countless bonfires, picnics, and dinners with new friends, and have found people down here that love to *laugh*.

Regarding the laughter: I've had the rough edges smoothed off of my own cynicism—cynicism and irony being equal parts a weapon, a shield, and sort of the sixth love-language in the North. I've learned that sometimes it's okay to be earnest.

I've lived and traveled a lot of places. I've holed up in apartments all over Eastern Europe, slept in a stone cottage in rural France, and called several cities home. And while I've loved aspects of all of them, for the first time in my life I'm not planning my escape. Jackson, oddly enough, feels like home.

An Open Letter to the Brand New Amazon Author Rank (Beta)

Dear Amazon Author Rank (Beta),

I appreciate the email this morning, alerting me to the fact that I am the 18,704th most popular author on all of Amazon.com, not to mention the 2,013th most popular in the "Religion and Spirituality" category. You really know how to make a guy feel good about himself.

You know, when I walk out the door each day to see that my neighbour's SUV seems to have grown larger and more magnificent overnight, or I have to go to a family function and listen to stories about cottage acquisitions, cruises taken, or new cars purchased, I'll just remember your email with fondness, realizing that now all I have to do to get a tangible sense for how I'm measuring up in this world is to look at the handy graph you've provided that charts my progress as an artist (updated hourly).

If only Ernest Hemingway and Sylvia Plath had one of these when they were around! I bet their careers would have been a lot more joyful, and I bet they would have been a lot less depressed. I bet Ernest Hemingway would have checked his Amazon.com Author Central Page daily, updating his profile picture and smiling at the upward trajectory of his line graph. Thank you Amazon.com.

As the 18,704th most popular of your authors—I know this comes with some clout . . . don't worry, I put my pants on one leg at a time just like you—may I humbly suggest some other rankings that would be helpful in my life? Perhaps your algorithms can help in these areas:

- **Amazon.com Tallness Ranking.** I'd like to know, definitively, how my height measures up to that of other popular authors. Am I taller than Steven King? How about the lanky but still elegant Garrison Keillor?

- **Amazon.com Body-Mass-Index.** Yeah, we're selling books, but are we staying fit? I mean sure, we can't buy sugar in New York City anymore, but what about the rest of us?

- **Amazon Net Income Ranking.** This one is pretty self-explanatory. Get on it, post-haste.

- **Amazon.com Ranking of Which Authors Were the Best Athletes in High School.** This one may be a little self-serving, but still . . . don't they say this is The Best Time of Our Lives? Let's *quantify* it! I mean really, how much of a contributor was Joyce Carol Oates on her high school volleyball team?

Well, I realize I've put a lot on your already-full plate, Amazon.com. No rush on any of that. Just know that I speak for artists everywhere when I say that it's a real privilege to literally be able to check our rankings hourly. I can only imagine how Picasso and Renoir would have been helped by something like this. Oh, the possibilities. If only you could somehow link my line graph to those other postmodern barometers of Success in Life—Facebook and Twitter. Then all my "friends" and "followers" could really see how well I'm doing.

Appreciatively,
Ted Kluck (18,704th Most Popular)

How We Talk About
the Things We Talk About:
On Disagreement Inside a Fishbowl

Originally Published in *The Jackson Sun*

When I was in college and immediately post-college, there were a few things about which I was insufferably smug. Because I had read like three books, start to finish, I was of course (in my own mind) an authority on nearly everything. Getting super mad not only happened often, it was fun! And I had way too much free time with which to roam around inside my own head as well as critiquing the headspace of others. What I really needed, more than anything, was a full-time job to make me tired and to take the edge off my insufferability. Thank God social media didn't exist in 1997.

That said, the 2016 Presidential election cycle and all of the hopelessness it contains, has cast a discernible pall over Union University's campus this semester. There is a certain brand of awkwardness and anxiety that is created when you, in an intoxicating fit of self-righteousness mixed with unprecedented cleverness, destroy a person on social media one evening, only to have to pass that person in the hallway and cafeteria four times the following day. Part of what is falsely emboldening about arguing on social media is the anonymity, except that when you go to a college where less than 2,000 people live on campus, there is no anonymity.

If you've spent any time around college students (or were one yourself) you know that college is a time for trying out personas—a few of mine included college football player, Soundgarden/grunge flannel-shirt-guy, and, later, social – justice – anti – consumerism – guy (which was without a doubt my most insufferable persona and, sadly, coincided with our wedding showers, meaning that we failed to register for anything cool).

All of that to say, identity is a huge deal for college students. And what makes me the saddest about right now was summed up well by a colleague who explained that we no longer simply attack a person's *ideas* but have taken to attacking a person's very *identity*. This makes these social media battles especially toxic and could make the fallout long-lasting and painful.

One of the coolest things about Union University is that it is an unapologetically Christian college where one doesn't have to be a confessing Christian to attend. It's not a requirement for admission. As per industry standard for all Christian colleges, there is lots of brochure-speak about the uniqueness of the community. I want this to be true. I want our community to be unique, but am adamant in feeling that it is only through Christ that we have a shot at a community where "grace" is not just an item of copy in a brochure, but is the actual outflow of continual broken-ness, repentance, and the conforming of our hearts to His image.

My prayer is that this would be evident in how we disagree. I think grace begins with not immediately ass-uming the worst of your classmates and professors. It's been my experience at Union that most Republicans aren't actually hateful misogynists, and most Democrats aren't God-hating pre-Communists. Nearly everyone I've met at Union is just trying to faithfully do a good job with what they've been given.

And I think it's incumbent upon those of us who identify with Christ to be willing to admit when we're wrong, and apologize. The older I get the more I'm convinced that this—apologizing—is actually the most rare, compelling, and winsome thing there is. It's how I'm continually reminded that Christianity is a real and hopeful thing.

I think repentance is our only shot at actually being a Christian college, and if this soul-suckingly-depressing election cycle offers anything, it is an occasion to repent of the mean things we've said or written out of a place of genuine frustration. It's a chance to extend forgiveness and grace in return. It's a chance to assume the best of a person, on the front end. It could be a chance to take a step toward the kind of community we advertise, but that has been in short supply in our culture.

February in Michigan is a Zombie Movie

"I didn't want to let February beat me this year," I said to my wife, re: February, re: depression, as I sat in our kitchen and nibbled a breakfast bowl of post-flu white rice followed by a chaser of Vitamin D caplets. February is the Dark Night of the Soul, in Michigan. It is gray skies, constant snow, and constant school cancellations because of wind chills (downwards of -30 in the mornings). February is what happens after a December and January about which you say, "It wasn't that bad . . . winter isn't that bad this year . . . I feel good! I can do this!"

February in Michigan has everyone stumbling around pale, wan, post-flu, or paranoid-pre-flu, making it not unlike a zombie film except that unlike in a zombie film, rich evangelicals can't just flee to Florida to avoid zombies like they can avoid the cold. "I think Florida is going to eventually fall off and sink into the ocean," said my father, in response to the fact that two-thirds of his church flees south every winter. It's just sour grapes, but still. I would flee south if I could. Incidentally, the same rich evangelicals usually go "up north" in the summer, meaning that they spend a grand total of about two weeks living where they actually live.

Note: If you're the kind of reader who reads a memoir and then goes to Amazon.com and posts a one-star review with the title "Too Whiny," then please stop reading.

Here's a partial list of things that have happened in the charming month of February:

- My pastor friend's church was robbed. Twice.

- Everyone in my house has had the flu, including my parents, who came to help because . . .

- My wife had surgery.

- We buried her uncle, who lost a brief but intense battle with cancer.

- I applied for a faculty job at the school where I adjunct that I really wanted and had the silly audacity to actually hope for, only to find out from my students that the new hire was in fact "really cool" and in fact "already on campus." My response: "I feel like burning a bridge."

The question is, "What can a person do with all of this February-related rage and disillusionment?"

Thankfully, I have good friends. Another pastor friend who is in the midst of some serious family-related struggles urged me to memorize Romans 15:13: "May the God of hope fill you with all joy and peace while you believe in him, so that you may abound in hope by the power of the Holy Spirit." That succinctly sums up my basic need. There are many other things I want (even need), but I still feel empty and hungry even when I get them graciously. It's like I can hardly enjoy anything without joy, peace, hope, and the power of the Holy Spirit, and I'm feeling greatly depleted in all of them.

I pray that for myself. I pray that for all of us. I pray that the "February" of our souls would be over soon . . . maybe even before the actually February runs out.

So Dope: Reflections on Indie Filmmaking

Originally Published in *The Jackson Sun*

My producer called the night before our production company was to begin shooting at the old Pontiac Silverdome in Detroit. "Both actors are in tears," he explained, "and people are being thrown out of hotel rooms." The line went silent for a moment as I tried to think of how to respond. "The good news is, this is happening now and not in the middle of the shoot," he said, ever the optimist.

I wrote a script a couple of years ago about a fictional ex-USFL quarterback who leaves his home, job, and family, in the midst of an existential crisis, to go and live as a squatter in the abandoned Pontiac Silverdome. The Silverdome was once the world's premiere domed venue. It was home to the NFL's Detroit Lions and the NBA's Detroit Pistons, as well as Super Bowl XVI, Wrestlemania 3, and many other sports and popular culture milestones.

I almost sold the script to an actor whose name you would recognize, who wanted to turn it into a concussion story—that is, to make the main character punchy and pitiable. I didn't want to go that route, so I hung onto it, figuring it was the end of my project. However, a year or so ago, shortly after moving to Tennessee, I showed the script to Glenn Pakulak, a former All-SEC and NFL punter and current actor, and he fell in love with the story and the character.

"I felt like you told the story of my life, and of so many former players," he said after reading it. "We have to make this." Glenn enlisted the help (read: funding) of several former NFL buddies, and soon we were forming an LLC, finding a producer and director, and setting about the herculean task of making a feature-length low budget independent film.

Today I'm reclining in a trailer, on the set of my own movie. It's surreal. Also in the trailer is Carmen Serano, best known for her work on AMC's critically-acclaimed show *Breaking Bad* and an unspeakably handsome young actor named Cisco Posada, who has a recurring role on Fox's record-industry drama, *Empire*. We're all marveling over the '90s-tech in the trailer, the most remarkable feature of which seems to be the sofa that mechanically slides back about six inches thereby, theoretically, "opening up" the living room of the trailer. Cisco is especially thrilled by this. "That is so dope," he says.

Chris Regner, our producer, is poring over budgets, and looking for ways to conserve cash, as is the lot in life of the indie producer. He lived in Hollywood for several years trying to write, when as it turns out, he was an incredibly gifted producer all along. I've known Chris for fifteen years; to see him excelling in this role is a thrill. In the back of the trailer, Thani Magnusson, a 2016 Union University grad, runs lines with Elizabel Riggs, another Union alum. They are former students, and it's a thrill to know them in this context—grown up and professional.

In a few minutes I'll go outside with my friends and we'll film a scene that I wrote, except that instead of little kids swordfighting in my folks' backyard, filming on an '80s CamCorder, we'll do it for real this time.

That is so dope.

Dear Guys My Age:
Nobody Cares about Your Diet

Originally Published in *The Jackson Sun*

One distinct memory of growing up in the 1980s is that my mom and her friends were always on diets and would always discuss their diets. Specifically, in the 1980s, fat was the *worst* (note: now fat is *great* and carbs are the *worst*) which led to my mom eating lots of dry-looking baked potatoes at Wendy's.

By contrast, I remember zero instances of my dad ever discussing his diet with any of his friends because I remember zero instances of my dad being on a diet, being excited about a diet, reading a diet book, or being especially worked up about his appearance. It fact, my dad's friend Dale was the first person who taught me that it's really tasty to boil bratwurst in a pot full of beer, with a stick of butter included. Cooking bratwurst in this way is the opposite of being on a diet.

Fast-forward to now. My age is in this range: I am older than 25 but younger than 43, but closer to the 43 end. And now, nearly every time I hang out with guys my age—especially guys my age who don't have an immediate bond-slash-thing-to-talk-about—conversation always turns to one of these things:

- Who is eating "clean."
- Who is in "ketosis."
- Who is cutting out carbs.
- Who is fasting in an intermittent way.
- Who is doing the Whole 30 or just a Half 30.

Here's the thing: I don't care at all about any of these things and, I'm pretty sure, neither do any of the other guys in the group (even guys who are doing one or more of them). We make obligatory comments like, "Man, you look great"[3] or, "Wow, that's interesting" or, "Yeah, when I 'ate clean' I immediately lost ten pounds but felt like killing everyone I encountered."

Note to all my guy friends: I'm glad you're healthy and I want you to be healthy and please don't feel weird around me vis-à-vis the fact that I wrote a column about how boring it is for us to talk about diets. Keep talking. Nobody change their behavior.

That said, it's a curious commentary on our culture. And lest this turn into a Comp 100 essay on "body image," let me just say that I do long for the days when men were less obsessed with their physiques.

My grandfather, who was mid-century-awesome and was, to be fair, blessed with a great metabolism, usually relaxed in the evening with a half a package of salami, washed down by a chocolate malted, washed down by an Alka-Seltzer or a Becks Beer if it was the weekend. I bet he read zero articles on diets in his lifetime. And instead of really exercising in a gym-or-Crossfit-way, he just sort of *did stuff*. He cared for his own lawn, fished, hunted, golfed, and played a bunch of baseball with his grandkids. Even at my tender age at the time, it felt to me like he was crushing life because he totally was.

I'm sad to report that he eventually died, as (news

---

[3] Which really means: "Man, you look like someone put one of those air-mattress vacuums in you and just, like, *deflated* you by 25%.

flash) all people do. I don't remember him slathering his body with hormone creams, taking little blue pills, or visiting any anti-aging clinics. He never dyed his hair in a sad way. He never had that odd moment that lots of current old guys have in that they look old from the neck up but weirdly jacked and steroidal from the neck down. I'm not even sure he thought about "aging gracefully," as a thing, so much as he just continued living the life he wanted to live, until he died.

It would be cool to also do this. Don't get me wrong, I want to live a long time to enjoy my wife, my kids, and, Lord-willing, grandkids someday. But I want to do so while also enjoying food, enjoying my hobbies, and not wasting another minute discussing my diet.

PART II:
POP CULTURE

Lady Bird and Oh My Gosh
I Hate Hipster Movies So Much

Originally Published in *The Jackson Sun*

I wanted to watch *The Mexican* last night and my wife wanted to watch *Lady Bird* so naturally we watched *Lady Bird*. Here's the plot of it, in a nutshell: a family doesn't get along and stuff happens and their eccentric daughter goes to college. *Lady Bird* is a really good movie that I hated.

During the movie you're treated to lots of scenes of the family not getting along and the girl becoming estranged from her best friend and then reuniting with her best friend and then not getting along with the mom and then having class-struggle issues and then very sadly and grimly losing her virginity (a staple of hipster movies!) and then . . . going to college. Of course, the girl was super clever and wise-beyond-her-years and wanted very desperately to leave her town and then when she leaves her town she wants to go back to her town. In that, she is every kid that has ever lived.

Also, the sad, estranged mom should have been Laura Linney but was somebody else. But it didn't matter.

The movie has telltale hipster movie stuff in it, such as a certain kind of slack-jawed delivery of lines, an obscure hipster soundtrack, older people from *That One Show* whose careers have been resurrected by the movie, an ironic reference to a pop song, people wearing cool hipster clothes, and a gay kid. These are all staple, non-negotiables. "Lady Bird" delivered all of these things. Also a depressed dad, which is a staple of every hipster movie. A depressed, slack-jawed, dead-eyed dad is an absolute *must* in these movies and is best when portrayed by Jeff Daniels. It wasn't him this time, but it didn't matter. Because it may has well have been.

These movies win awards at festivals. These movies don't get viewed in theaters. These are the movies you invoke the names of in order to look smarter. In this, they serve a very important smugness-related purpose.

So there's nothing really big happening in these movies. Nobody is stealing anything or killing anyone or playing any sports or winning any wars or aspiring to anything. There's nobody you'd want to be. Nobody is trying to be a singer or a getaway driver for heists, and nobody is trying to open a jazz club.

Here's what there is, though: a small house that somebody is ashamed of, some rich kids who are shallow, a pool party, and some class struggle. There's a depressed priest who teaches theater who is being treated for his depression. There's for sure somebody working "double shifts" and somebody wearing scrubs but not being a doctor. Make no mistake about it, though: this isn't fun. In spite of the main girl's propensity for calling herself Lady Bird, and in spite of her funky dye job and her standard-issue-freshman-art-student wardrobe, there is absolutely nothing fun about this.

There's somebody who's conflicted about who he/she is or where he/she is from. The gay kid is for sure crying when he gets caught kissing another dude.

This isn't a bad movie. As pieces of art go, I guess it's great. The script is great and is super clever. When people are saying lines, you take note of how clever they are. The

cinematography is really nice. Sacramento looks nice in it. It's the right kind of hipster-sad. It does everything right. There's nothing escapist about it, though. It will remind you, sadly, of your own life, your own failures, your own shallowness, and your own broken relationships . . . but not in a way that gives you any hope.

So here's how to use this movie: in the right kind of crowd, you can really make yourself look better by talking about *Lady Bird* in a certain way. Take note of its ironic use of a Dave Matthews band song that everybody actually loves. Talk about how it's a love letter to Sacramento (itself, ironic). Talk about how you were "totally Lady Bird" in your high school (subtext, you were smarter, cooler, and less-shallow than everyone else).

So, in conclusion, watch the great movie *Lady Bird*; you'll hate it!

Bill Haverchuck is Innocence Personified

Originally Published in *The Jackson Sun*

You know that feeling you get when you've discovered a great television show to stream, yet are nearing the end of those precious episodes? The feeling is a sort of low-level grief over the fact that this will never be "new" and you won't be "discovering" it anymore. It's also the feeling that you will soon have to replace the show with another show that may not deliver the joy and escape and warm feelings that your current show is delivering. In fact, if one were to lay this pathology over, say, the life of the serial monogamist, he/she would probably feel/experience the same things. But that's not the point.

I'm in the midst of this feeling with the 1999 high school television comedy *Freaks and Geeks*. The show originally aired during a year that I spent living in television exile, in Lithuania, so I missed it the first time around. It takes place in a high school in suburban Detroit in 1980, and despite the fact that a good half of the characters dress and style their hair in unspeakably 90s ways, it captures the nostalgia of the 80s perfectly (not unlike *Stranger Things*). But my grief over almost losing the show isn't the point either.

There's a particular character in the show, Bill Haverchuck, who is, legitimately, a nerd but also wildly compelling to me. The word "nerd" has been co-opted in the last fifteen years by actual cool people claiming to be nerds, which is really disheartening. I think Rivers Cuomo, from Weezer, started this. But Bill is a nerd in the sense that he is awkward, gawky, has bad teeth and hair, and bad glasses. And he hangs out with uncool people—at least per the social calculus of high school in 1980.

Bill is captivating to me because looking at him is like looking at pure, distilled innocence. Bill is innocence personified. Here are a few ways in which this is true:

1. He is uneasy and recoils when given the opportunity to view pornography in Neil Schweiber's basement.

2. He truly seems taken aback when he becomes intoxicated drinking the beer in Sam Weir's room—which beer the boys confiscated so that nobody at Lindsay Weir's party would get drunk and make bad decisions. Bill was just thirsty and thought it would quench his thirst.

3. Bill is a friend to all, as evidenced by the way he treats Gordon Crisp, as well as the other nerds in his group.

4. Bill is a loyal and courageous friend, as evidenced by the way he has Sam's back when the group is jumped by Alan White's posse—which is interesting in that Alan White is, himself, not much further up the social food chain than Bill Haverchuck.

Even Bill's apparent moral failure—like prank-calling Coach Fredericks (who totally deserved it)—results in Bill's hero moment: he stands up to the coach, demands that the geeks be allowed to choose sides in softball, and then makes a Willie-Maysian catch on a fly ball. The thing about Bill is that (in his own mind, and maybe real life) he is sneaky-athletic.

His face is the picture of openness, innocence, and joy (especially while eating—which he sort of does with an open mouth, but not in a gross way). I hate that the show had to end after 18 episodes but am thankful I didn't have to see the slow march of innocence-robbing time that would have inevitably happened to Bill, as it happens to us all.

It's a reminder that shows ending can be a mercy. The fact that I didn't have to see Bill lose his virginity, marry the wrong girl, smoke weed for the first time, or get fired is actually a comfort. What's hard about real life is that it's a series without an elegant ending, and a series in which I sometimes don't like the main character very much (me). It's a reminder that my character needs a little more Bill Haverchuck, and a little less Jerry Seinfeld (clever), Sam Malone (smooth), and Frasier Crane (smug).

Everybody Look at Me Saying,
"Don't Look At Me"

I had an interesting conversation with a friend today, regarding whether there will someday be a definitive *burst* to the social media bubble, wherein we all realize:

a. I'm bored with myself—and by "bored" I mean everything from actually just bored to semi-disgusted by my own narcissism to actually fully-disgusted by it.

b. I'm bored with the people in my life—including the stuff above about being semi or actually-disgusted.

c. Either social media doesn't actually help me sell the products I'm trying to sell, or it actually does but the process of doing that (i.e., being That Guy, i.e. the constant posting) isn't worth it and makes me feel creepy.

d. "I wonder what happened to the last decade?" which is ironic inasmuch as my social media platforms have given me the vehicle by which to archive the last decade in images, pithy sayings, movie quotes, links, and songs. But by "I wonder what happened to" I mean how might I have redeemed that time minus Facebook, Twitter, Pinterest, et al.

I told my friend that probably in a decade or so there will be "Social Media Ruined My Life" memoirs and also

Oxford-University-Press-Type examinations of social media written from a past-tense perspective. Of course, the past-tense-perspective thing means that either a.) it's just over, or b.) there's something else to replace it.

My friend ruminated that for the first time in ever we have (via social media) the means by which to place a numeric value on the things that people have wondered in high school cafeterias since the beginning of time (postfall), which is basically, "How much do people like me-slash-how many people like me?"

I responded that the ability to place a numeric value on this is probably going to shipwreck our collective character, regardless of which side of the scale (popular or un) we're on. And if nothing else, social media is a great revealer of one of our culture's main idolatries: the praise of men.

We finished by wondering if someday, someone will be able to graciously decline fame. We realized we'd never actually seen anyone do this, as the only options tend to be either completely punk-rocking it and dropping out (see: Salnger, JD) or at least keeping your audience really small *or* embracing fame whole hog (see: too many people—Christian or "secular"—to count, including, at some level, all of us via social media).

The problem with completely punk rocking it is that you only get one shot at making your point and then after you've made it you can't really make any other points for fear of risking your credibility and being thought a fraud.

We decided, ironically, that it will take somebody really famous (in the right circles) to basically say "I really appreciate all the attention, awards, pats on the back, etc., but with all due respect (and I mean that), stop looking at me and I will in turn stop using my fame to move product."

Anyway, I give it another decade before we're left with an emotional black hole where social media used to be (and before all the memoirs and Oxford Press books come out).

Movies You're Required To Say You Like But Probably Actually Hate: *Fargo*

Fargo is a movie that cool people usually like. It's a Coen brothers movie, and it generally gives you some artistic cachet and says some things about your own character (funny, envelope-pushing, etc.) to say that you like Coen brothers movies—which is, if you think about it, the reason we talk about the pop-culture that we like (saying stuff about ourselves). I had managed to go through all of the '90s and '00s without seeing *Fargo,* and was reminded by some podcast co-hosts that this was a problem. So I watched it.

It has Steve Buscemi (who I love), Bill Macy (who I like), Frances McDormand (who I love from *Almost Famous*) and is about a kidnapping/multiple-murder situation that actually happened in and around the metro areas of Fargo, Minneapolis/St. Paul, and Brainerd, MN. It didn't actually happen, of course, but there is text on the screen claiming it did.

Here's the premise of *Fargo* in one sentence: Isn't it funny to juxtapose a bunch of horrible, dark, grisly stuff with the general cheeriness and funny accents and quaintness of the upper Midwest?

This is, admittedly, a funny conceit . . . but it's really only funny the one time. When it's kind of the only trick of an otherwise pretty grim/depressing movie, one is left to wonder why *Fargo* garnered the success that it did? McDormand and Macy were both great, as they nearly always are. Macy's character was pitiable and sniveling

but also endearing in the certain sad way that people are sad when their fathers-in-law turn them into whipped puppies. McDormand was great even though this particular character didn't have much in the way of dimension. Buscemi's character was awful, which was the point. He and his sidekick were chilling reminders of the quick, downward slide of sin and deceit. They killed a bunch of people, ultimately, because they felt like they had to not get caught. That part was sad.

So I guess I had trouble yuk-yukking about the Nordic accents and quaintness when at the same time a bunch of innocent (and probably otherwise nice/harmless) people were getting very graphically slaughtered. I remember feeling the same way about watching *Pulp Fiction* for the first time as a pretty sheltered 19 year old. What's weird is that I'm not at all sheltered now (probably to a detrimental degree) but *Fargo* gave me the same feeling.

Granted, there was funny slaughtering happening in *Django Unchained* and *Inglorious Basterds*, both of which I loved, but it was generally (broadly) purposeful. There was a sense of justice to both of those ultra-violent-but-also-ultra-clever movies.

I really hated *Fargo*. The cleverness (which was really there) didn't make up for the darkness, which was also abundantly there. This movie was off the charts on "total depravity of man" and very low on "created in God's image."

Jason Momoa's Amazon Prime Movie *Braven* Could Resurrect a Genre

Originally Published in *The Jackson Sun*

"Wanna watch this Jason Momoa movie, *Braven*?" I asked my wife. She knows my Momoa-related man-crush issues. If I could look exactly like any living person, it would be the actor Jason Momoa who is best known for playing a super-jacked guy with awesome-looking hair and tattoos who never had to speak, on *Game of Thrones*.

She, surprisingly, assented.

"Let's give it ten minutes," I said, figuring that within ten minutes I would have my curiosity assuaged and realize that I wasn't missing anything. Except that what happened is that it was decent (not great—decent) and a reminder of a genre that I used to really enjoy: the '80s/'90s paint-by-number action movie.

We finished the movie in a tidy 94 minutes and she really enjoyed it. Here's the formula for a great '80s/'90s action movie, which is a genre that I now hope Momoa singlehandedly resurrects:

- Have an awesome-looking guy who may or may not be steroidal and may or may not be very good at acting (see: Seagal, Steven; Van Damme, Jean-Claude; Statham, Jason). Being a skilled actor doesn't really matter as it pertains to these movies.

- Put that guy in a scenario in which he has to protect somebody or multiple somebodies who are clearly vulnerable. In the case of *Braven* this is Joe Braven's dad (who has dementia) and his daughter. Also, the name Joe Braven is real and wasn't just made up by me for comedic effect.

- Have a character with a name like Joe Braven.

- Have a really sinister and one-dimensional bad guy and reveal very early on just how sinister and one-dimensional the bad guy is by having him (probably) kill someone in a way that seems senseless and excessive to all involved.

- Have one or more of the vulnerable people do something that is momentarily heroic. This is really important. Have the daughter call for help. Have the demented father kill a bad guy. You get the idea.

- Have a script with a surprisingly good plot, and dialogue that is really mediocre in the following way: it only ever moves plot, and never reveals character.

- Make sure that script is no longer than 90-95 pages. If these '80s/'90s action films roll on for close to two hours, it's too much of a good/bad thing.

- Never have anything preachy or social-issues-y in your script.

These are the kinds of movies which, in 1991, I used to ride my bike to the video store in the summer to rent on VHS with my buddy Russell. We rented them because they were 94 minutes of fun escapism that allowed us to view a version of what some guy in Hollywood deemed "bravery." The good guy always won. The vulnerable people were always protected. There was never any art-house agenda or "deeper meaning." The movies weren't intended to "make you think." The hero never died.

In 2018 the vast majority of movies are either based on a comic book or a video game. This trend is, I hope, getting boring for people and is also almost over.

What these '80s/'90s action movies provided was a succession of "new" characters (He's a logger! He's a cook on a cruise boat! He's a pastor who is an ex-Marine! He's a hot priest who fights crime at night!) presented in a comfortingly predictable format.

The final piece of the formula is an ending in which the hero kills the bad guy in a way that is super creative and that you, the smarter-than-average movie-watcher (or 9th grade boy), couldn't have thought of on your own. *Braven* delivered this and it involved a bear trap—but not in the way you might think.

Restraint is Cool: In Praise of the BBC's *Pride and Prejudice*

Originally Published in *The Jackson Sun*

Let's get something out in the open right away: there's only one adaptation of Jane Austen's classic novel *Pride & Prejudice* that I ride with, and it's the BBC's version starring Colin Firth and Jennifer Ehle from 1995. This bad boy weighs in at a whopping 327 minutes, so you're looking at several evenings of premium entertainment.

Why do I ride only with the BBC *Pride & Prejudice*?

- It takes that long to really tell the story.
- Only a real woman, like Jennifer Ehle, can play Lizzy.
- Nobody can do smug-but-ultimately-good-hearted like Colin Firth.
- Alison Steadman as Mrs. Bennet.
- Restraint, both in storytelling and actual behavior of people. More on that later.

I met my lady in 1995, and this DVD set has been a part of our lives for nearly as long as we've been together. Our viewing cycle usually goes like this: after several nights of action, comedy, and sports (I have two sons), my wife wants to watch something with some combination of the following in it (preferably all): British people, dresses, Colin Firth, Jeremy Northam. Perfect examples in this wheelhouse include *Gosford Park*, *Downton Abbey*, and almost every Jane Austen adaptation, but especially *Emma* and this *P&P*.

There's this great scene that happens shortly after Charlotte Lucas has married Lizzy's bloviating idiot cousin, Mr. Collins. What happens is that Lizzy goes to visit Charlotte at Rosings Park, and Charlotte brilliantly indicates in the scene that she is both happy with her arrangement (per that time period, her material needs are provided-for) but is also happy to see the repellant Collins as little as humanly possible. "He spends a lot of time in the garden, and I encourage him to go for several long walks each day," she explains to Lizzy, who doesn't push for more information but who, rather, totally gets it because she is smart and intuitive herself which is, by the way, part of what makes her super attractive.

We live in a hot-take culture. You don't have to look hard to find people verbally destroying each other on Twitter or Facebook. Nor do you have to look hard to find people trying shamelessly to look sexy, funny, rich, accomplished, available, athletic, knowledgeable, exasperated at the President, supportive of the President, or some combination thereof. Every day. Over and over. The aggregate result of this is, typically, exhaustion and depression and the sense that if a giant meteor were to, say, hit the planet at full speed and destroy it, it wouldn't be the worst thing.

That said, the BBC *P&P* has a restorative effect. I love how their definition of a "good day" is one in which you read a book and walk around the garden. I love how Austen, as only she could, takes a hammer and blasts away at smugness-for-no-reason (Collins, Bingley's sister), social-climberness (Collins, Mrs. Bennet), lack-of-a-backbone (Mr. Bennet), stupidly throwing yourself at a sexual predator (Lydia Bennet), and being that sexual predator (Mr. Wickham).

And I love how Darcy just quietly solves a whole bunch of problems for Lizzy and her family, making him super attractive as well.

Televised entertainment today is lurid and over-the-top—what with flesh-eating zombies, meth dealers, corrupt politicians, and glamorized lawlessness ruling the day. It's also, in some cases, extremely well-done. That said, I think there will always be a place for a quiet story, with timeless character motivations, well-told. And I can't think of a better way to spend a Saturday night with my lady.

'90s Movies that Aren't Actually '90s Movies: *500 Days of Summer*, Zooey Deschanel, and Self-Awareness

I recently re-watched half of the movie *500 Days of Summer* with some college students. It's a movie I remembered really enjoying in 2004 (it actually came out in 2009) in that it was very clever and broke the "romantic comedy" mold. I also really enjoyed this half of it but for different reasons.

What's interesting about watching it now is that it occurred to both of us that 2009 was sort of right at the beginning of the hipster movement, inasmuch as being rampantly self-aware-slash-"nerdy" (but actually really hot and cool) was becoming a "thing" right around then. *500 Days of Summer* can be best described as a bunch of cultural references and self-awareness ("I love The Smiths!") with a little bit of a movie thrown in.

It also occurred to us that Zooey Deschanel is the physical embodiment of self-awareness in that her movie characters always have a very carefully curated persona (vinyl records, 50s dresses, ironically eating at crappy diners, liking Ringo Starr, hating the job, etc.) and don't seem apologetic or even the slightest bit sheepish about this. Her characters are not unlike the carefully-curated online personas of nearly everybody now. 2009 was close to the beginning of that phenomenon too.

Driving home, we had a conversation about Deschanel that went something like this:

My wife: "Do you think she's hot?"

Me: "I used to . . . but her character's rampant self-awareness actually makes her less hot."

In that, she's sort of a girl version of Wes Anderson in that I love his movies but I'd always be nervous that I was liking the "wrong" thing around him, which would make hanging out laborious and awkward. What's funny is that, in a way, this is how the movie plays out, in that the (spoiler alert) Joseph Gordon Levitt character was never quite good enough for her. It's '90s in that it plays with chronology a la *Memento* (still the best Chris Nolan picture), has the thing where a 24-year-old working a low-end job has a Manhattan apartment worth $1.5 million, and also the thing where the 11 year-old little sister is the preternaturally sage voice of wisdom.

That said, *500 Days* is still an almost perfect movie in that it's just sniffy and dismissive enough about romantic comedies so as to satisfy the too-smart-for-everything-ers and it's enough of a rom-com to satisfy everybody else.

Jack Reacher, Pete Mitchell, and Ethan Hunt Are All the Same Person and They're All Awesome

Originally Published in *The Jackson Sun*

For no good reason, I recently viewed *Jack Reacher: Never Go Back*. It's the latest in a long line of Tom Cruise Retirement Tour action films in which he plays an old man still doing young man action film things. Despite the 43% score it received on Rotten Tomatoes, it may have actually been one of the most perfect action films I've seen, in that it had lots of (for the genre, at least) nuanced character stuff to go along with the Cruise staples, which include fighting, running, and hanging off of things.

Decades ago, when Cruise first aggressively chomped gum, played homoerotic volleyball in jeans, and asked to use his girlfriend's shower on his first date as Navy fighter pilot Pete "Maverick" Mitchell, he cemented a character which would become his go-to well into late middle age: the rebellious military guy . . . meaning the guy whose rebelliousness is initially abrasive and off-putting, but whose creativity and out-of-the-box thinking ultimately allow him to be heroic, causing the older authority figures in his life to both ruminate on how much of a pain-in-the-ass he is and ultimately assent to his particular brand of rebellious brilliance, be it in flying a jet (*Top Gun*) or fighting, running, and hanging (the other ones).

Cruise is really the only action star who delivers this particular thing. Harrison Ford's (and most recently John Krasinski's) Jack Ryan character was always the good guy thrust into the bad situation, Jason Bourne made a franchise out of being confused about his own identity and wanting to make it (the identity) stop, and John McClane (*Die Hard*) made a franchise out of being unusually awesome at doing a pretty common thing—being a regular cop in a series of outrageous terrorist situations.

The Hunger Games
Made Me Cry like a Little Girl
(and Other Theological Dilemmas)

Startling Admission: I just finished book three of The Hunger Games trilogy, and I am a simpering, quivering, teary-eyed mess. I—author of books on Mike Tyson and Pro Football, sparring partner to a pro heavyweight fighter—have been reduced to a Dick Vermeil-ian/just-watched-*Beaches* level of tearfulness by a piece of young-adult fiction. [pauses to sniffle, grab Kleenex]

Okay. Better now.

The question is: why? Here's the thing: I know what books I'm "supposed" to feel strongly about and this isn't one of those books. I'm "supposed" to say that *The Hunger Games* is an inferior version of *Lord of the Flies*. I'm supposed to sniff derisively (not tearfully) about a piece of young adult fiction that shouldn't worm its way into my home, shouldn't worm its way into school curriculums and definitely shouldn't worm its way into my smug, too-good-for-everything, MFA-educated heart.

Except that it did.

The Hunger Games won't worm its way into any school curriculums, as long as PhD types continue making the decisions about such things, and as a result, your kids will continue to complain about the boring books they have to read in school and skip their reading assignments, in much the same way that we complained about the boring books we had to read in school and skipped our reading assignments. The fact of the matter is, if somebody had a gun to my head and said, "You can only read one book before you die, for entertainment, and it has to either be *The Hunger Games* or *Lord of the Flies*," I'd choose *The Hunger Games*.

Why *The Hunger Games* Is Working as Popular Reading

1. It has girls (which makes it different from *Lord of the Flies*; see: female audience, importance of; see also: *Twilight, Harry Potter*).

2. It has a story that's far-fetched but not too far-fetched. It's set "in the future" but not too far in the future. Everything that happens in it is big, sweeping, and outlandish but not so big, sweeping, and outlandish as to never be plausible/feasible in real life.

3. It was impeccably and relentlessly marketed. Let's be honest—this matters. Do I ever want there to be a "companion piece / movie-viewing-guide workbook" published alongside one of my books? The artist in me says, "Of course not." The bill-paying part of me says "Absolutely. Bring it."

4. As outlandish and blood-bathy as the storylines are, they deal with motivations that we all have—and pretty much hit every one of Maslow's Hierarchy of Needs: Physiological (food, clothing, shelter), safety, love, esteem, and finally self-actualization. It's all in there, and those needs tend to make for pretty interesting characters.

5. I read my fair share of fluffy entertainment, but I also read my fair share of smug, too-good-for-everything, pinky-out, serious *lit*-erature, and this works as both, in my opinion. There is a mastery of plot, and a mastery of writing here that good books have both of. Suzanne Collins will never be mistaken for David Foster Wallace but she's not trying to be. If *The Hunger Games* was written as her MFA thesis, her committee would be fawning all over it.

6. Disdain-for/distrust-of the government.

7. This is a book that is "doing it" for teenage boys, middle-aged ladies, adult males, and pretty much every other demographic imaginable. That, alone, makes it interesting. The only other thing you'll see more copies of being carried around airports are boarding passes.

Make No Mistake, This Thing Really Is An Absolute Bloodbath

If you're a parent deciding whether or not to let your impressionable youngster read the books, make no mistake, this thing is a full-on gorefest. I'm a fan of gangster literature, and have consumed my fair share of Godfather and Elmore Leonard novels, and this is gorier than any of those are (body-count wise), despite being packaged and sold as "young adult fiction." The only thing "young adult" about these books is that they star a seventeen-year-old main character. But, like *The Godfather*, they deal with universal (and therefore interesting) human themes and experiences. Also, for what it's worth, the third one, *Mockingjay*, is by far the bloodiest. At one point I almost bailed on it.

The Concept of the Secular Savior and *Why The Hunger Games* Ultimately Doesn't Do Anything for Us on a Spiritual Level Except as a Vivid Illustration of the Doctrine of Total Depravity

Finally, there is the question of whether *The Hunger Games* does/should do anything for us as Christians. If you've read any of my other stuff you know that I'm pretty big on entertainment and good writing just for the sake of entertainment and good writing.

Not all entertainment specifically comments on *how* we are saved/redeemed as people, but good art generally makes us think about it, and this book does. Except that it's wrong. We're *not* saved or redeemed by other peoples' goodness or our own goodness. And we're *absolutely* not redeemed by someone loving us, with the singular exception of that Someone being Jesus. This, of course, is where these books break down for us as believers. But what's weird about these books is that they're all trying to create a human Jesus—the kind of character that embodies all of the goodness and hope that we as humans can imagine. The only flat, one-dimensional character in the series ends up, of course, being the Human Jesus character.

I won't give away the last page of the last book, which pretty deftly lays out Katiniss's personal theology. Spoiler Alert: It's a sad and empty personal theology, though it's also the kind of personal theology that could masquerade as hopeful to a mass audience. Also, it made me cry, and that's something I guess.

Ultimately, what the book does do well is that it gives us yet another illustration of depravity at work. The idea that man, unleashed and left to his own devices, is capable of massive amounts of evil, selfishness, and evil begetting more evil. Evil done to man, outside of the redeeming salvation of Jesus, just creates more evil. Only Christ and the Cross can break that cycle. Only forgiveness can break that cycle. As humans, we deal with that ourselves each day. We don't want to forgive; we want to punish. But if everyone insists on punishing to the degree that we've suffered, we end up in a *Hunger Games*-style emotional bloodbath. Only Christ saves us from that.

So is this article just another smug Calvinist taking the joy out of everything, as Smug Calvinists are often wont to do? No way. Read *The Hunger Games*? Absolutely. But read it with an eye toward who you are, in Christ, and on who Christ is for us.

On *A Star is Born* and the Grossness of Fame

Originally Published in *The Jackson Sun*

I loved *A Star is Born*, starring Bradley Cooper and Lady Gaga. It was nearly perfect, as movies and stories and characters go. And I saw it at the Plaza Theater in Humboldt, Tennessee, which is nearly perfect as theaters go, with my wife, who is nearly perfect as people go.

At one point about two-thirds of the way through the film, I leaned over to Kristin and whispered, "I'm sorry for wanting to be famous." She understood exactly what I meant.

I used to want fame. It's a thing I distinctly remember verbalizing once, to a friend of mine, when we were in our early twenties and feeling full of ourselves. He asked me if I would rather be rich or famous. I picked famous without even thinking about it. I wanted people to ask for my autograph. I wanted to be asked back to my high school to give a graduation address. I am ashamed of the amount of time I spent thinking about those scenarios.

A Star is Born is about the grossness of fame more than it is about depression or substance abuse (and it is also about both of those things). Cooper is perfect[4] as the grizzled, older rock star who has tasted of fame and found it unable to heal the hurts and fill the voids in his past, and in his heart. Gaga is perfect as a young, talented girl who still thinks fame is worth pursuing, despite his attempts to

---

[4] Shame on me for seeing *Wedding Crashers* in the early-2000s and thinking that Cooper would peak as an '80s-movie-style D-bag like the one he played in that movie. I was wrong. He's amazing.

warn her. Sam Elliot[5] is perfect as the Cooper character's older brother-slash-manager and perhaps the most-grizzled person to ever walk the planet.

They are both right, and they're both wrong, which is what is perfect about the film. He loves her with a love that is unbridled and childlike and sweet, and is jealous of her when her career spikes. His embarrassment—for her and *by* her—is evident when she takes her pop-star turn on *Saturday Night Live*. It is as evident as her horrified embarrassment when he—loaded—urinates on himself onstage at the Grammies.

It's fame—the spiking of hers, and the maintenance of his—that really provides the engine for this film. It provides the engine for the sweet, had-to-be-autobiographical moment with Dave Chappell's character in which he describes his journey out of the limelight, and into peace. Chappelle's speech, after Cooper has passed out on his lawn in Memphis, may be my favorite part of the film.

This movie is really about how fame, and love, are both inadequate to redeem a life. It's a tough message, but a good and honest one.

When I was apologizing to Kristin I was apologizing for all of the narcissism and greed and neediness-for-approval which came along with the chasing of fame. It turned me into the kind of gross person who was always curating a persona—often to the detriment of those around me. I cared more about the opinion of "the world" (by which I mean a few book critics and nameless/faceless

---

[5] At what age did Elliot first turn the corner from young to grizzled? I'm guessing fourteen.

Amazon users) than the opinion of the people in my own home.

Like the Cooper character's substance abuse, I'm not sure anyone is ever fully "cured" of the fame/persona disease because, at his essence, man was created *to* worship and not to *be* worshipped. However, the fight is easier because of films like *A Star is Born*. Walking to my car on the quite nighttime streets of Humboldt, I thanked God for my modest job, my family, and the relative monotony of my day-to-day life.

Love, Grief, and *Peace Like a River*
Originally Published in *The Jackson Sun*

For about a decade I avoided reading a novel called *Peace Like a River* by Leif Enger. I avoided it because I was convinced it would be depressing (it isn't) and also because I was afraid that the author would be better than me at doing something that I've always tried very hard to do: writing about faith in a way that is raw and genuine and authentic and vibrant but not preachy or heavy-handed.

I picked up the book in the midst of some pretty heavy early-semester glumness this weekend. I always get glum when the school year starts—not because I don't love teaching (I really love it)—but because each year I'm presented with a new batch of young, idealistic, dream-addled, energetic students (which is great) while each year a little bit more of me has been worn away by the natural degradation of adulthood which includes, but is not limited to, money stuff, relationships that are hard, the ever-dimming flame of my athletic life, and creative projects that are moving more slowly than I'd like.

Aside: my students actually seem to like it when I get glum. I don't think they've had much experience with adults who show actual non-Instagrammable emotions and, to them, there is a certain romantic, '90s-esque appeal to my dark periods. One time they brought me some '90s self-help books and a sad turtleneck and they can almost always be counted on to bring coffee. All of this totally helps.

Reading Enger this weekend made me realize that I've

chosen my past literary heroes very cagily. David Foster Wallace wrote like a wild animal—style and swagger and smartest-guy-in-the-room jumped off of every page—but it never threatened my heart. As much as I loved and was inspired by Wallace over the years, it was the resounding gong or the clanging cymbal. Ditto for Tom Wolfe, J.D. Salinger, Charles Bukowski, and Jim Harrison who got the closest in *Legends of the Fall* but still never quite got there.

In *Peace Like a River* Enger writes about faith in a way that shows what actual faith looks like. He writes about prayer in a way that makes me want to pray. He writes about being a father in a way that actually makes me want to be a better father.

"I love this," I told my wife last night. "But I could never do this . . . I'll never write anything this good." She then said something very sweet about how we're different writers and that's okay. She can always be counted on for this kind of encouragement, which is just one of many reasons why nothing compares to her.

But rather than being grieved that I didn't write *Peace*, I dove back in. I let it speak to my soul. I thanked God for it. Maybe this is a sign of maturity. Maybe adulthood isn't so bad after all.

Ted Interviews Himself about Jordan Peele's Fantastic Movie *Get Out*

Originally Published in *The Jackson Sun*

I don't watch horror movies, due to a very traumatic experience that took place when I was in 7th grade, involved the movie *The Silence of the Lambs*, and was also my first date. Long story. For that reason, I am very late to the "Writing Affectionately About Jordan Peele's *Get Out*" party in that I just watched it last night.

Don't let being a total wimp about scary movies, like me, come between you and a viewing of *Get Out*.

What is *Get Out* about, and how is it not a horror movie?
Well, it's about a black guy (played by the wildly charismatic Daniel Kaluuya) who's dating a white girl, and has to go and meet the affluent suburban family of the white girl. Which, in addition to being weird in the normal ways (meeting parents, subtle racism, etc.), is also weird because it turns out that said parents (both doctors) are into some really dark, proof-of-man's-total-depravity and man-trying-to-be-God stuff. Tense moments ensue. It's not horror because while there are jumpy moments, and in the last fifteen minutes it leans on (and is an homage to) some tried-and-true horror movie tropes, it's not, primarily, about scaring the viewer. I would call it a psychological thriller, as opposed to a horror movie.

Who is Jordan Peele?
Peele is a filmmaker, writer, and comedian who is perhaps

best known for his Comedy Central sketch show *Key &
Peele,* has made two brilliant movies already, and is also
younger than me. A fact which I'm not at all jealous of?

**How long before you knew you were watching some-
thing brilliant?**
Two minutes. The first scene was impeccably paced and
shot, and set the perfect tone for the rest of the movie. I
knew I would love it and I did.

**Does this make the age-old dilemma of being an out-
sider tangible and understandable?**
It does. And while I have no idea what it's like to be black,
I have very much been an outsider at times, and have felt
those "pit of my stomach" outsider fears. I also remember
what it was like to visit my wife's family for the first time
and while I wasn't specifically afraid that they would hyp-
notize me and saw into my skull, sometimes it felt like
they wanted to.

Did you feel preached-at at all while watching *Get Out?*
If there's anything I hate, it's preachy movies. If I wanted
to be preached at in a heavy-handed and non-clever way,
I would just log onto Twitter rather than watching a
movie. That said, I felt zero percent preached-at by *Get
Out.* While it is manifestly thoughtful and does address
some social issues, I felt like I was just being told a great
story laden throughout with invitations to think and
connect.

What do you mean by "wildly charismatic" re: Kaluuya?
He communicated a lot with his eyes only. And he was entirely sympathetic while also being real.

But, re: the preaching, isn't it a satirical critique of black/white relations in America?
Well, yeah, but primarily it was a searing commentary on the awkward things white people say and do to not appear racist. And I guess I appreciated Peele making those jokes in a way that gave me (a white guy) permission to both acknowledge and laugh at the awkwardness. And it totally succeeded (in my house, at least) at raising issues and igniting conversation, while also managing to not take the fun out of the story itself.

Did the creepy, affluent white surgeon (the girl's dad) totally remind you of somebody you know in terms of both personal aesthetic and manner-of-speaking?
Yes.

Well?
No, I'm not gonna say.

Did you like this better than *Black Panther*?
Well, they're different movies, and liking movies isn't a zero-sum game, meaning that if I like one movie, I don't have to hate the other one. That said, in my opinion *Get Out* is a way better movie than *Black Panther*.

In skewering liberal, white cultural-elites, isn't Peele running the risk of making fun of the self-same people

who would (theoretically) champion his movie and use it to make themselves look cooler?

Yes. The fact that he doesn't grab the lowest-hanging comedic fruit possible (the Trump joke) is part of what makes this so brilliant. As is the fact that white, liberal, cultural elites are still going to champion the movie. It's just that good.

London Boulevard, Gangster Ethics, and the Dark Heart of Sin

"As for you, you meant evil against me, but God meant it for good, to bring it about that many people should be kept alive, as they are today."

Genesis 50:20

You probably shouldn't watch *London Boulevard*, which stars Colin Farrell (who really can act; see: *In Bruges*) and Keira Knightley. It was also written and directed by a writer and director (William Monaghan) who was cool enough to have written *The Departed*. The fact that it has a super cool Brit-pop soundtrack (Yardbirds, Stones, and some Bob Dylan who is cool enough to have been made honorarily British at some point in his life), is relentlessly artful without being fey and annoying, and has the only satisfying ending that it possibly *could* have are additional reasons why you shouldn't watch it.

Actually, it's great.

Here are the disclaimerish reasons why you shouldn't watch it, and then two more reasons why I found it super interesting:

Disclaimerish: It squeezes about 1,200 f-bombs into 103 minutes, people do drugs, other people get shot. There's the obligatory 15-second strip-club scene which it seems all modern gangster-type movies must have. Now you know. So don't watch it and then say, "I was surprised by all the profanity and violence."

Now, onto the real content.

The writer/director probably meant this film for evil, but I think God meant it for good. Let me explain. The Colin Farrell character just got out of prison and is trying to be a Good Guy. Farrell is absolutely genius at playing the "conflicted bad guy who just can't quite seem to stop being bad even though he really wants to be good" (see: Bruges, In). Still, Farrell gets roped into his old life because of some commitments he's made to his boss, who is a gangster and who, even though he's British, reminds me a lot of Gene Hackman. Farrell inevitably falls in love with Knightley, who's a reclusive famous actress (in the film). Of course, Farrell is pursued by his gangster boss, who sees great potential in him and wants him to take on more criminal responsibility, to which the Farrell character replies, "See, what you have to understand is that if I were a gangster—Rob—you would be the first to die. I wouldn't work for you. I would kill you and take everything you've got—if I were a gangster. That's why you don't want me to be a gangster. Nobody wants me to be a gangster. 'Cause I couldn't stop if I started. Do you get it?"

Hence, the Gangster Ethic. Most gangster movies show how cool this ethic is, and how much it works if you are just steely, motivated, poised, and ruthless enough to pull it off (see: Corleone, Michael). This film does the opposite. It shows the Gangster Ethic for what it really is, which is full of dissatisfaction, paranoia, crippling guilt, and pain. Which is why the Farrell character wants out.

In short, it shows the Dark Heart of Sin for what it actually is, rather than the way Hollywood usually portrays it, which is consequence-free and awesome. This is a film full of people getting what they deserve, and instead of making you feel great (as an audience), it makes you feel sad and empty.

In a strange way, this film made me glad that I know Christ, and that I don't have to live by the Gangster Code in my life or my career . . . and make no mistake, we all (especially men) live by it in one way or another at some point or another. We all want to be God. We will all fail at being God. The Bible guarantees this, and even if you don't believe in the Bible, all one has to do is open one's eyes in the world for a few minutes to see how horribly this goes most of the time.

This film did no business. It barely got distro in America, doing a paltry $3,400 gross on opening weekend— scarcely enough to fund Colin Farrell's hair product. It came and went because on paper it's just another depressing art-house picture where everyone dies (Spoiler alert, I guess, but you knew that anyway didn't you?).

But at the end of the day, it made me glad to know the Lord.

A Grand Life: On Beauty, Rest, and *The Phantom Thread*

Originally Published in *The Jackson Sun*

"We've had a grand life," whispered my wife, Kristin, as we watched Daniel Day-Lewis driving through a little European hamlet that was similar to the little European hamlet we once lived in.

As phrases whispered by girls in dark movie theaters go, this has to top the list. In lots of ways, I'd been waiting twenty years of living, working, writing, husbanding, etc. to hear her say that. I wanted—for reasons ranging from mostly selfish and childlike to occasionally noble and sacrificial—to give her a grand life.

So *The Phantom Thread* is supposedly Day-Lewis's last picture. In yet another symmetrical twist, marriage-wise, his character in *The Last of the Mohicans* was college-aged Kristin's paradigm for what a real man should be. She wasn't wrong, and I've spent the better part of twenty years trying to be that man—a lover, a fighter when necessary, the owner of a great head of hair.

In *The Phantom Thread* he plays Reynolds Woodcock, a famous London dressmaker who is utterly devoted to his craft, weirdly relational with his stern sister, and a confirmed bachelor. He's also sometimes insufferably rude and smug and idiosyncratic, in addition to being suave and charming.

Spoiler: Every single outfit Day-Lewis wears in the film is the single greatest outfit you will have ever seen in the world, up to that point. Even his pajamas. It's as though the actor said, "Dress me in the most amazing things you can find, because this is how I want to be remembered." Ditto for the dresses, and the women, and the cars. This is a gorgeous film to both look at and listen to. Each establishing shot is a painting, and even the sound design is a delicious pleasure. The sound design is so rich that the crackling fire you make in your own fireplace after viewing *The Phantom Thread* will disappoint you compared to the fires that Reynolds Woodcock made in the movie.

It's not a spoiler to write that Woodcock, of course, finds love . . . in the form of a young woman who stands up to his bullying in some subtle and not-so-subtle ways. If you've seen the film, you know the not-so-subtle way I'm referring to. But I would argue that the subtle ways were more significant. And this much is true: she *loved* Woodcock's work and was eventually as devoted to the craft as he was. The scene where she stood up to a boorish client and insisted that said boorish client return a dress because the client wasn't worthy of it, was my favorite in the entire film. And it acted as the confirmation of her love and devotion to Woodcock.

It's also not a spoiler to suggest that she went to some, uh, *drastic* measures to see that he slowed down and rested and depended on her. The drastic measures were, at best, psychologically-twisted, and at worst morally-indefensible but about such measures I have, in the past, said to my wife Kristin, "Sometimes I wish somebody would just . . . " If you've seen the film you know what I'm referring to.

What I was really saying, in those moments, was: "I

wish I could just collapse and hit the reset button in a dark room for 48 hours, where nobody wants or needs anything from me." What Woodcock and I really need is rest and margin. What we need, sometimes, is to depend on someone else, which is the opposite of a sign of weakness.

The beautiful thing about the film is that it says these things much more subtly than I just said them. So subtly, in fact, that in the midst of all the psychological intrigue, it would be easy to miss.

As I type this I'm sitting under a framed arrangement of photos and paintings that we've collected in twenty years of grand living and travel. It's the kind of arrangement you make, of course, when you want people to think you've lived grandly—the pictures of Prague and Jerusalem and the Black Sea and western France. The kind of image-curation that Instagram has employed to turn most citizens of the world into the most insufferable versions of themselves. But to be completely honest, in between the grandiosity, for us, has been lots of grinding and toil and sometimes frustration.

Watching Reynolds Woodcock made me thankful that my refinement—the smoothing off of my rough edges and work obsession—has been less severe, and that my lady has been much kinder about it. It really has been grand, from the coast of France to a dark movie theater in Jackson on a Saturday night.

Driscoll, Pop Culture, and Trying to Sound like Chuck Palahniuk

Background: So I was recording "The Happy Rant Podcast" last night and I was asked about the latest Mark Driscoll controversy which I basically knew nothing about because I'm basically not on the Internet (meaning not on Twitter, Facebook, Instagram, or EmergentVillage.com). And I'm not on the Internet, in part, because of stuff like this. That said, if you want to know the nature of the controversy, simply Google "Mark Driscoll William Wallace."

I woke up this morning to an email from a friend containing links to some of the online ranting done by Driscoll in the early-aughts under the pseudonym "William Wallace II." Knowing this friend, the idea behind the email was simply to provide a little levity . . . though coming on the heels of the podcast, it seemed like a good time to figure out what was behind the latest kerfuffle. What it is is some grade-A unedited semi-crazy Internet ranting, the likes of which felt kind of new and original back in the late '90s when we all "had a voice" because of the quote/unquote Miracle of the Internet.

Anyway, I read the ranting, the content of which wasn't all that interesting. What was interesting was the obviousness of the link between Driscoll and pop culture, which made me think about how much we are all influenced by the books we read and the movies we watch.

Like about two-thirds of all white Christian males in the early 2000s, Driscoll clearly had a fascination with Mel

Gibson's William Wallace character. Because it's been a while since *Braveheart*, I can't quite remember how we all made the link between painting our faces, wearing a kilt, charging down a hill to kill about 2.5 thousand people with an axe, and Christianity . . . but we somehow did.

The other thing that was alarmingly clear to me about Driscy's ranting was how badly he was trying to sound like Chuck Palahniuk, author of *Fight Club* and probable ruiner of lots of undergraduate writing in the late 1990s. Driscy was not alone in trying to sound like Chucky P; I tried to sound like him for a while, and so did (again) probably every youngish white male in every MFA program everywhere. The Palahniuk link was there in both content (be a swaggering masculine badass at all costs), and style (be short, staccato, and purposefully un-beautiful, because being beautiful is for our wives and also for pansies).

Those two movies, for whatever reason, pretty much perfectly encapsulate the late '90s. Interesting that they were such a heavy influence on Driscy's ranting. Which begs the question: Is it wrong or bad or dangerous to identify that much with a piece of pop culture? I mean, Driscy would still essentially be the same guy without *Fight Club* and *Braveheart*, right?

Luckily, for me, I find much of my identity in *Rocky IV*, which is everything great about everything, including parenting, politics (ending the Cold War), marriage, race (Rocky's best friend was a black guy), cars (don't drive your Lamborghini angry), music (lots of songs about hearts that are on fire), and sports (cheaters lose, even if they look awesome like Drago).

Everybody's Nose Got Bulbous: How *Mission Impossible: Fallout* Reveals Cultural Attitudes on Aging, Marriage

Originally Published in *The Jackson Sun*

Let's be clear on one thing: I really liked *Mission Impossible: Fallout.* It was exactly what a movie "like that" is supposed to be—two-plus hours of explosions, car chases, fight scenes, people hanging off of cliffs, people chasing each other in helicopters, and gunfights. It delivered all of those things and I had a blast watching it with my wife and kids.

However, watching Tom Cruise, age 56, hanging off cliffs, fighting in bathrooms, sprinting a whole bunch, and trying to seduce hot girls in their late twenties, I was left with the same awkward feeling I would feel if, say, a bulbous-nosed favorite old uncle was trying to do the same things. Something along the lines of, "Unc, why are you doing all that at your age? Why don't you sit in a chair and regale me with stories, or dandle a grandkid on your knee, or do what other normal 56-year-olds are doing?"

For the sake of perspective, old actor Jon Voight was roughly Tom Cruise's age *now* in one of the earlier *Mission Impossibles.* However, if someone had said, "You're going to watch a movie where a 56-year-old Jon Voight fights, sprints, jumps, climbs, and seduces all over the place," you would have laughed him/her out of the theater. And rightfully so. Even the apple-cheeked "kid" in the MI triad, Simon Pegg, is now 48 years old.

This phenomenon (old people doing young-people things) is proof of two things:

1. **We can't age gracefully**. In *Fallout*, Alec Baldwin was the only actor who was truly allowed to be an old person with actual wrinkles and actual gray hair. Conversely, watching a fleshy, jowly Cruise, 56, hang off the side of a mountain after a lengthy helicopter fight was the same as watching a fleshy, jowly, middle-aged Muhammad Ali fight Trevor Berbick at the end—it was proof that whatever "this" is, it is in fact over. My favorite scenes in the movie were the scenes in which Cruise, for a few minutes, channeled his Jerry Maguire character. I would love to see him doing more of this, in more movies.

2. **We have a generational lack of male movie stars**. The fact that all of our coolest actors are nearing retirement age—Pitt, Denzel, Clooney, Cruise, et al—but are still being cast in actiony roles. This is proof that male movie stardom skipped a generation. Heck, even our favorite icons of Millennial Slouchiness are now 30 (like Michael Cera). The fact that Cera's generation of movie star didn't produce anyone who was capable of believably carrying a gun onscreen is, perhaps, why we have a 56-year-old Cruise hanging off a cliff.

The film also had interesting things to say about marriage. I guess that what I'm about to type is a "spoiler" of sorts, but it's not terribly central to the movie's main narrative and, also, you don't go to see *Mission Impossible: Fallout* for the story arcs of secondary characters . . . so read accordingly: Cruise's wife in the franchise has remarried a JC Penny model who is also a doctor.

You'll recall that while Cruise's character was busy carrying the weight of the world on his slouched, middle-aged shoulders, and playing God, his wife went into semi-hiding and, in fact, remarried. In the film this was couched in a sort of "See, it all worked out in that I'm doing exactly what I was *supposed* to do, while you're doing the very thing (playing God) that allows me to feel safe as I fall asleep next to this cheekbony JC Penny model each night."

This was something the audience was supposed to feel good/encouraged about inasmuch as, culturally, marriage is seen as a fluid, ever-changing exercise in each of us "reaching our potential," happiness-wise.

As you can probably tell by my less-than-respectful tone, I disagree, in that I see marriage as a covenental and lifelong bond which makes me about as relevant, cul-turally, as a covered wagon and a pair of burlap overalls. Oh well. As a heterosexual white male who is nearing middle age himself, I understand the fact that nothing I say is "right" and everything in the world is my fault. I get that, and it's okay.

I guess I would have loved a *Mission Impossible* in which Cruise ages gracefully with his wife of 20-plus years, while maybe missing an opportunity to "do some-thing amazing." I think, as people, we miss a lot while we are chasing "amazing" opportunities. However, in that, maybe what I'm longing for is *On Golden Pond* which doesn't exactly quicken the pulse or pack the theater on a Saturday night.

So Tommy, shine on you wrinkly diamond—we'll see you again in a couple years.

Why I Love Raymond Reddington's Character but also Why That Character Could Never Exist in Real Life, in Light of Romans 1

I am newly addicted to *The Blacklist*, in which Ray Reddington (portrayed ridiculously well by James Spader) is a hardened and very successful career criminal who seems to have a newly-acquired heart of gold. In short, Reddington (chief among criminals) avails himself to the FBI to aid in the catching/killing of other awful criminals for a variety of purposes, the first of which seems to be the level of closeness it affords him to agent Elizabeth Keen, with whom he has a complicated relationship.

The thing about Reddington is that, per the show's exposition (and also per what happens in every episode), he has killed, extorted, and fornicated around the world and continues to do so with a smile on his grizzled-but-handsome face. But he also seems to have an equally strong need to "do good" but not in an assuaging-guilt sort of way, which is the usual reason why people want to "do good" if they aren't in Christ. Reddington, on the other hand, seems to have very little actual guilt, in that he continues in the behaviors which one would normally feel guilty about. His reasons for wanting to do good are more complicated.

The other thing about Reddington is that he is devastatingly clever, funny, strong, capable, and well-connected. He is suave and worldly, and seems to know everything about everything, but not in a way that makes him insufferable (as it would with most people). Every woman in his orbit wants to sleep with him. Every guy is both a.) scared of him and b.) completely entertained by him. Reddington is like a funnier and less tragic Don Draper. He's the guy you always wanted to be (minus, of course, all of the killing, pillaging, and sin).

Another thing about Reddington is that he is probably the reason for a lot of regrettable fedora purchases over the past few years. The thing about you is that you can't wear a fedora like Reddington/Spader, so don't even try. But I digress.

Something that's bothered me about Reddington is the fact that, per Romans 1, there is no way this person could exist in real life. And this truth is, in fact, a comfort. The first chapter of Paul's letter tells us of the hardening effect of sin over time, and of the chilling way that God eventually gives some people over to their sins—their hard hearts, their unchecked lusts, and their depraved minds. It's honestly one of the scariest things in Scripture because it precludes the hopefulness that the Reddington character dangles in front of us in each episode.

Those passages are meant to ignite in us a radical change of heart—a reliance on Christ alone, and a turning away from those things that harden our hearts. Reddington is, in a biblically-unreal and impossible way, having it both ways on a grandiose scale. Now, to be honest, I am in smaller ways trying to have it both ways too—in that I struggle each day with my sinfulness and am far from the man I want to be in Christ. But what's weird is that Reddington seems to continue in embracing/loving his sin, but also embracing his newfound hopefulness/gentleness. Per Romans 1, this could not be.

This is, I guess, what makes fiction fiction—the fact that it can't happen in the same way that Superman isn't real. The Blacklist is great fiction.

Revisiting Michael Mann's 2015 Disaster, *Blackhat*

Originally Published in *The Jackson Sun*

One of the last things I did as a Michigan resident in 2015 was viewing Michael Mann's film *Blackhat*, which stars Chris Hemsworth and is about cybercrime. That fact that in the '90s Mann directed *Last of the Mohicans* and *Heat* gives him a lifetime of goodwill from me, even though *Ali* was pretty bad after the first eight minutes (which were brilliant, and Will Smith was brilliant throughout) and *Public Enemies* could have been a lot better.

Note: In spite of what I'm about to write, I still think Michael Mann and Chris Hemsworth are great at what they do.

When I viewed *Blackhat* in 2015 I thought it was terrible, as did most people who saw it. So it's strange, then, that I watched it again last night and did so with the same sense of hopeful "it has Chris Hemsworth and Michael Mann—how bad can it be!" anticipation I brought to the film the first time.

My interest in the movie was rekindled by a podcast I listen to on the Ringer Podcast Network called "The Rewatchables" in which they reference Mann and *Blackhat* often enough (with a mixture of derision and admiration) that I thought it deserved a second watch.

I was wrong.

Blackhat took itself seriously but totally shouldn't have. However, it offers an interesting master class in how to make a bad movie. Consider the following steps:

1. Take a handsome and wildly-charismatic actor (in this case, Hemsworth), and put him in the one haircut (part-'90s hair, part-high-school-softball-coach) that makes him look terrible.

2. Take that same actor, who is Australian, and make him do a really terrible New York accent which (accent) has absolutely nothing to do with the character or the story. His character could have been from anywhere and the story doesn't change at all.

3. Put that actor on screen opposite an actress with whom he has zero chemistry. Then make them sleep together for absolutely no reason except that they are a man and a woman who happen to be together in the same room a lot. Hemsworth had way more chemistry with Viola Davis, for what it's worth, and I think that relationship would have really had a shot.

4. Make the actor do all kinds of shots where he just sort of sits there and thinks, and do so with the requisite atmospheric Michael Mann *Heat*-type music playing in the background. There are plenty of actors who can do sitting-and-thinking and pull it off (see: Hardy, Tom, who has made a career out of this). Hemsworth isn't one of them.

5. Take an actor (Hemsworth) with a super physical presence and make him do the following: sit behind a computer terminal and type while sometimes uttering the words "malware" and "mainframe" and "network." I'm sure cybercrime is a really interesting thing to ex-

plore, but when your movie's chief "action" involves writing code and your movie doesn't involve kids in the '80s hacking into computers to either a.) manipulate their grades or b.) launch missiles, I think it's time to re-think your cybercrime movie.

6. Include a super-long gunfight scene for almost no reason, and then make the gun sounds very loud and the dialogue very quiet.

7. Spend $70 million on your movie, only to see it gross $8 million.

Watching Michael Mann's *Blackhat* is really an exercise in watching a John Woo movie but without the self-referential fun-factor (see: lots of slow-motion jumping and dove-releasing). John Woo, deep down, knows he's making fun, crappy movies and I respect him more for it.

Also, Brad Pitt did *Troy*, which should make Hemsworth feel better if/when he runs across *Blackhat* on cable in the near future. It's also a reminder that if movies are supposed to be fun, sometimes it's fun to watch a bad one. Watching Hemsworth trying to do a Brooklyn tough-guy accent was fun in the same way as watching the super-hot guy in your high school trying to take the ACT.

Blackhat succeeds if only as a reminder that even really talented people sometimes miss the mark as mere mortals, like me, do often.

If the Bradys Were a Reformed Family

In a fit of nostalgia, I recently picked up a couple of seasons of *The Brady Bunch* on DVD. I'm enjoying the walk down memory lane and, for some reason, my boys find this show captivating in spite of plot vehicles such as "Cindy has a secret admirer who is actually (spoiler-alert) Bobby," and "the homeless-looking guy at the Grand Canyon who locks you in the jail cell actually wants to be your friend and share the gold he finds in the abandoned town with you."

It occurred to me that The Bradys are, in some ways, a Reformed-ish family. They spend a lot of time together. They have six children. They're concerned with leading a certain kind of moral life.

Here are the ways the show would change if the Bradys were a Reformed family:

- Davy Jones would be replaced by Lecrae.

- The trip to the Grand Canyon would have actually been a trip to the Laura Ingalls Wilder estate in South Dakota and on the way there they would swing up through Minneapolis to hear Piper preach (full disclosure: we took that exact trip two summers ago and it was awesome, though I also wish we had also gone to the Grand Canyon and been given Native American names a la the Brady Family).

- Joe Namath would be replaced by Tim Tebow.

- Marsha's skirts would be longer and less fashionable.

- Greg would spend less time talking about his many girlfriends and more time thinking about whether those girls were of a level of character commensurate with that of a Proverbs 31 wife. Also, he would already be married to an aforementioned Proverbs 31 wife but only after an extended courtship during which he was careful to include his parents and siblings.

- It goes without saying, but that would eliminate any Marsha-related sexual tension.

- Instead of a dog, the family would own chickens in order to teach the children responsibility and also to get cheap eggs even though, ironically, eggs are still pretty much the cheapest thing you can get at the grocery store.

- The chickens would die because the lawn is made of Astroturf.

- There would be more Scripture visible in the home and less of Mike Brady's arrogant architectural flourishes. In plainspeak, the awesome staircase and the different levels in the living room wouldn't detract from the glory of God, because they wouldn't be there.

- Mrs. Brady would actually do something, and not just let Alice do all the work.

- Mrs. Brady homeschooling would eliminate any plot vehicle including: friends at school, being or not being the school president, being or not being the captain of the football team, being or not being popular, being or not being a cheerleader (immodest anyway), getting or not getting Davy Jones/Lecrae to perform at Prom.

- There wouldn't be a prom. Instead, there would be a banquet where people still get dressed up and eat, but there's no dancing.

- Alice would be younger, and as such would work for less money. But she would still be an old spinster, even at age 23. She would still make quippy, but not bitter, jokes about her singleness.

- Mike and Carol's bathrobes would be more modest.

- Mike would spend less time doing the following: returning home from shopping trips (?), sitting at that sweet desk but not appearing to do any work.

- . . . and more time doing the following: blogging, trying to get a book deal.

- Sam the Butcher, Alice's love interest, would actually take some initiative in the relationship rather than just stringing Alice along in the way that he's currently stringing her along. Also, he wouldn't be a butcher, he'd be a seminary student with an acoustic guitar and a large collection of theology books—many of which he hasn't actually read. He would be under the tutelage of a Wise Older Man at his church who would be encouraging him to play less Xbox and hurry up and marry Alice.

- As such (above), Greg and Bobby wouldn't have gotten trapped in the meat locker at Sam's shop, robbing us of one of the best episodes in the history of the series.

Creed 2 is Bad and It's Okay
Originally Published in *The Jackson Sun*

Here are three truths: Michael B. Jordan is amazing. Tessa Thompson is amazing. *Creed 2* is a bad movie.

I saw the film in a packed theater in Nashville with my son and nephew on the day it came out. I have an unabashed love for the *Rocky* franchise and celebrate all things related to it. I loved *Creed* and thought it was the second-best film in the entire franchise, after *Rocky* itself (Best Picture, 1976). I had high hopes for *Creed 2*.

When the film finished and the end credits rolled, everybody sat there for a couple of beats, and then someone clapped, and then a few more people clapped tepidly, because the cultural expectation is that you clap at the end of a Rocky movie. But in our heart-of-hearts, we all knew that we had just seen a very mediocre movie.

Yet the cultural headspace we're in doesn't allow us to acknowledge that Michael B. Jordan can do something bad. Such is the nature of an audience's love affair with a transcendent young actor. But the thing is, all great actors occasionally do bad movies. Brad Pitt did *Troy*. Robert DeNiro did *Dirty Grandpa*. Sylvester Stallone did *Rocky V*. And *Creed 2* not working wasn't at all Michael B's fault. Here's what was bad about *Creed 2:*

1. Stallone regressed from the awesome old-man-ness he embraced in *Creed*, and he went back to looking tan and waxen and like a very old man who was trying really hard to look less old.

2. Every Stallone line had a fortune-cookie-wisdom Lifetime Movie quality about it which made it feel inauthentic and forced. The script just wasn't that great.

3. It was 20 minutes too long.

4. Ivan Drago, the villain from *Rocky IV*, was actually the most sympathetic and interesting character in this movie, which removed a fundamental element from the success of any Rocky movie—hatred for the opponent. Drago and his son were so sympathetic (on account of his wife, Brigitte Nielsen, leaving him high and dry after his defeat at the hands of Rocky and the end of the Cold War in 1985), that I almost wanted them to win the final fight, get Drago's wife back, and bring the Drago family back together again.

5. None of the emotion the viewer was clearly *supposed* to feel felt earned and authentic like it did in *Creed*, in that Rocky's son, with whom he had supposedly reconciled in *Rocky Balboa* was suddenly super estranged again.

6. It suffered from a lack of Ryan Coogler directing.

That said, it did have its moments. The training montage in the desert was cool. Tessa Thompson singing her husband into the ring for the final fight was a chills-producing moment.

This may be the end of the franchise and that is also okay. It's not a disastrous, ultra-embarrassing end, like we all feared *Rocky V* could have been. It's just a quiet, forgettable end. And I think our culture needs to re-find a "gear" in which something can be neither "amazing!" nor "garbage!"

Michael B. Jordan will, hopefully, go on to do dozens of amazing and important films. This just won't be one of them.

I Wonder if Wes Anderson Ever Gets Tired of the Wes Anderson Aesthetic?

We're halfway through our first viewing of *Moonrise Kingdom*, which is the latest in the Wes Anderson oeuvre and is, like the others, extremely 'Wes Anderson' in its meticulously stylized sets that look like they came from what thrift stores would look like if they had thrift stores in heaven . . . which is to say that they're perfect. Whoever gets to do set design, combing the country for the perfect orange rotary-dial phone to go with the perfect ironic plaid pants—all for one five-second scene—is one lucky hipster.

That said, I'm a veteran of all of the Wes movies. I love them all, and I own them all, though during the opening frames of *Moonrise* I thought I detected the initial pangs of being tired of the Wes Anderson aesthetic. I have no idea if this is normal. There's no one in my real life with whom I can talk about such things besides my wife and, truth be told, I'm a little afraid to hear her Wes-related opinions, unfiltered, as I'd be afraid of the comparisons I'd be tempted to make (see: Jealousy, below) between Wes and myself.

As the camera predictably moved us (the viewer) through a cross-section of the Bill Murray character's house, in all its '60s-ironic-ecelctic-slightly-disenfran-chised-but-still-cool glory, I felt like I'd seen the frames before (I had, in *The Royal Tenenbaums* and *The Life Aquatic*) and thought that perhaps I might be sort of thinking about being tired of them. I chalked this up to either:

1. **Artistic Jealousy.** Anyone who has ever tried to do anything arty but has failed because of any combination of lack of budget, lack of audience, lack of talent, etc. has to be at least a little jealous of Wes Anderson, who gets to make arty, funny movies that are mainstream enough so as to get real budgets, attract real stars, and get made at all. He's living all of our dreams. In my mind, when I think of most filmmakers, there's something significant enough about them that I don't like as to make me not feel jealous of them. Not so with Wes.

2. **Aesthetic Jealousy.** This one is different, in that it simply speaks to the fact that I like all of the houses in the Wes movies (the boat in *Zissou*, the houses in *Tenenbaums* and *Moonrise*) way better than my own house inasmuch as my own house doesn't have rotary phones, period-specific record players, books with ironic covers, art that's supposed to be bad but is actually awesome, and all manner of sulky but attractive people living in it.

3. **Bill Murray Jealousy.** He gets to basically sulk and be disenfranchised for the duration of each Wes Anderson movie he's in. I'm jealous because when I sulk and am disenfranchised in real life it doesn't come off nearly as charming and winsome as it does when Bill Murray does it in the movies. Perhaps it's because my real life lacks the right obscure Brit-pop backing tracks. Or perhaps it's because real-life sulking is sort of awkward and off-putting for the real-life people in your real life. Either way, I need to work on this.

I wonder what Wes Anderson's house looks like? I wonder if he has a secret, muted, unrequited desire to sometimes gorge himself on Jerry Bruckheimer action films and bad '80s hair metal? I wonder if there's anything tacky about his house? I'd be glad and relieved if there is, but also a little disappointed if that makes sense.

Aside: As I type this I'm wearing a "Baumer" t-shirt written in FILA font, which is a tribute to the tennis player Richie Tenenbaum, aka "The Baumer," who fell in love with his adopted sister Margot in *The Royal Tenenbaums.*

The Wes Aesthetic, in a dialogue sense, is always saying the right thing and even if it's the wrong thing it sort of comes off as the right thing. Again, this is something I'd love to pull off in real life but have trouble actually doing.

In a plot sense the Wes Aesthetic involves putting lots of interesting and troubled people together, sort of nibbling around the edges of really dark themes, and then somehow having a virtue like Charm (all of them) or Love (*Bottle Rocket*) or Family (*Tenenbaums, Mr. Fox*) or Wounded Charm (*Zissou, Rushmore*) rule the day to such a degree that the story can end and even though what we've seen has nibbled the edges of being dark and arty, we don't feel like we've seen an art film, which is to say that we don't feel depressed.

In this, the Wes Aesthetic is almost like a religion. It's one that, granted, ultimately doesn't work and that I may already be starting to be sick of, but still . . . it's like a religion.

Argo and Infinite Jest

One of my favorite books is a novel called *Infinite Jest* by David Foster Wallace. Caution: I'm gonna get pretentious here for a second . . .

Anyway, one of the many storylines in Infinite Jest (which you should read) is about a film that is so compelling that anyone who views it is so enraptured by it that they can't eat/sleep/bathe/etc. and therefore they eventually die. The film falls into the hands of some terrorists, stuff happens, etc. Interestingly, the book was written in the mid-'90s but is set in the "future" which is actually now-ish. Some of the stuff that happens in the book is purposefully over-the-top and jaunty, but some of it could actually/is actually happening.

One of Wallace's goals for the novel was to write a challenging, literary, avant-garde book that was, in a way, as compelling as the movie the book was about—meaning that when you were at work you were thinking about *Infinite Jest*, you couldn't put it down at home, etc. This was my experience both times (I've read it twice).

That was a long introduction to the movie *Argo*, which by now everyone knows is great. To me, *Argo* reached an *Infinite Jest*-level of being compelling. Now, it's not news to be emotionally manipulated by a movie, because all of the great ones do this (manipulate). What was different about *Argo* was complexity and layering of the emotional manipulation and the comprehensiveness of the emotional buy-in.

Various things I said to my wife during the viewing of *Argo*:

- I want to go to a military recruitment office after this, and enlist."

- "I want to do something great with my life."

- "I want to never leave the house again for any reason, because of how scary/broken/dark the world is."

- "I wish every scene had Alan Arkin in it." (this is true—he's absolutely hilarious/amazing in every scene he's in.)

The point is that *Argo* had such a significant emotional/spiritual pull that I found myself praying, semi-subconsciously, that the people on the screen would make it, then realizing I was praying for a situation that didn't actually exist in the here-and-now and in fact took place over 30 years ago.

Questions we discussed after Argo:

- How would knowing Christ change/color your reaction if you were in a situation like the one they were in?

- I wonder if the film's portrayal of Iranians/Iran upset anyone?

- Did the fact that we adopted internationally and had some of the same (albeit less intense) traveling-internationally-in-a-hostile-place intrigues color the way we viewed the film and/or how deeply we bought in? (It did.)

Anyway, you should see it. See it for all of the above reasons, as well as the '70s fashion (hot), '70s music (Zeppelin), retro phones (awesome), retro ashtrays (saw like three that I want now), locations (I had never realized Iran was actually beautiful), Alan Arkin (the man), and Ben Affleck (also the man; see also: *The Town*).

The Only Safe Thing on Television:
Monty Don's French Gardens
Originally Published in *The Jackson Sun*

I stumbled upon a Netflix show that is none of the following: racist, sexist, homophobic, liberal, or conservative. It is not a commentary on anything, nor does it invite you to think about any "deeper issues." Nobody gets killed, nobody gets made fun of, there are no zombies, and there are no affluent, burned-out, disaffected middle aged men deciding to produce drugs, sell drugs, or run drugs, as is all the rage nowadays.

The last decade of dramatic television taught me that, if you're bored in your career or your family life, the answer isn't to work on positively changing any of those things; rather, it is to enter the fast-paced and exciting world of narcotics!

There are no insufferable couples looking for a home together. Nobody is acquiring, flipping, or cleaning a house. There is no false enthusiasm. There is no domestic violence. Absolutely no one is being objectified.

The show is *Monty Don's French Gardens* and its premise is as follows: Monty Don drives around and looks at gardens in France. Big gardens, impressive gardens, humble gardens, food gardens, chef's gardens, and roof gardens. Gardens are cool, France is a cool-looking country — seems like a simple enough premise for a great show that will offend absolutely no one.

If you like lots of lush, decadent photography of flowers and vegetables, you'll like this show. If you like seeing people enjoy nature, enjoy eating, and enjoy each other, you'll like this show. If you like seeing a guy who is relentlessly positive and encouraging but is also in no way cloying or fake, you'll like this show.

Nobody is falling into or out of love. Nobody is being given a rose or being asked to leave an island. There are no survival scenarios.

I suppose, if the show has a weakness, it's that Monty Don is an older white man, but the fact that he's British makes that okay, probably? Because older white British men are immune from ever being oppressors or bigots or bad people in any way. I learned this, primarily, from Bill Nighy, Colin Firth, and the dad from *Pride and Prejudice* (the BBC one). All three of those men are stand-up guys.

Nobody is laundering money.

If Monty Don has any unusual sexual proclivities or unpopular political opinions, we're not getting them in this show. What we are getting is Monty Don complimenting people on their gardens, and meaning it. Don harvests, tastes, and makes-much-of a variety of fruits and vegetables, in a variety of places.

The show isn't a low-key call to a vegetarian lifestyle. The show isn't a televised sport, and as such there are no head injuries, controversial halftime shows, or polarizing political statements. Zero elite high school athletes announce their college choice on *Monty Don's French Gardens*, and the show is better for it.

If you're into watching an older guy drive an older Citroen around the French countryside, you'll be into this show. If you want to see that older guy stop at a ditch and find a dead body and then examine some bullet casings, you'll be disappointed. It isn't that kind of show.

Get Low and Works-Based Salvation

Get Low stars Robert Duvall and Bill Murray and defies easy categorization. It's definitely not a comedy, though it is occasionally funny, and it's definitely not a drama although it is full of dramatic moments. Duvall plays an old, creepy hermit who lives on the edge of town and of whom everybody in town is scared. Rumors abound about him killing people or having killed people. Bill Murray plays a mortician in a town where everybody is young and nobody is dying. He (Murray) drinks too much and is depressed because he seemingly can't succeed at the only fail-proof business known to man. *Get Low* is quirky, but it's a different kind of quirk than the Wes Anderson kind. It's sort of quietly and gently quirky in such a way as to suggest that it doesn't want you overwhelmed by the quirk.

So the Duvall character's problem is that when he was young he did something horrible—and for the sake of not spoiling the movie I won't reveal what it is but it involved a woman he wanted but couldn't have—and while he was afraid to confess his sin before God and men, he decided to build himself a cabin on the fringes where he would live out his life in a de facto prison of his own creation. As you can imagine, the guilt and bitterness eat him up to the degree that by the time the movie starts he is old and ready to come clean (kind of). Except that he still can't really bring himself to come clean, so he plans a funeral event (while he is still alive). The Murray character is happy to oblige because it represents a massive payday and lots of publicity for him.

The funeral takes place on the Duvall character's property in front of a capacity crowd of tailgaters and curious onlookers, as everybody wants to know what's up with the old freak on the edge of town. A local pastor implores Duvall to confess his sins before God and men, and receive Christ's pardon, as this will be the only way to continue living without misery and also the only way to die in a right relationship with God, echoing Paul who writes in Romans 1 that the gospel is, "the power of God for salvation of everyone who believes." Except that Duvall doesn't believe and, in fact, believes that the only way to "atone" is to continue in misery. This is a very human impulse and is, in its own perverse way, a variety of works-based salvation. In this case the "work" being my own flagellation of myself. In its own way it denies God's goodness and God's power to save sinners, "of which I am the worst" (again, Paul).

What Duvall does is grab the mic and sort of "report" on what actually happened. He does admit that it was his fault. He asks forgiveness for not saving the girl, to whom something terrible eventually happened (meaning, her death—I don't know why I'm trying to be coy about that). He doesn't seek forgiveness for the sin that caused the horrible thing and in fact does a good bit of justifying of the "love" that motivated it—love being a sort of secular "greatest good" in the sense of "conquering all" and all that. After his half-confession, the movie implies that he can now die in peace and is in fact shown at the end walking toward the woman he couldn't have.

As Christians we know that this isn't true, and we

know that the guilt and misery he had to live with was actually a call to repentance. In that, the film was beautiful. It was also beautiful just because it was beautifully shot, paced, written, and acted. But the sad part of the film was its justification of the Duvall character's self-justification.

It's sad because self-justification doesn't work.

Wind River is a Great Film but a Bad Movie

Originally Published in *The Jackson Sun*

Jeremy Renner's semi-action/semi-murder-mystery/semi-drama *Wind River* got a lot of positive raves from the smart people in my life who talk about movies. Written by Taylor Sheridan, the film is set in Wyoming—but in the bleak, desolate sense of Wyoming (i.e. loneliness/despair) rather than the romantic sense (i.e. the mountains representing how life is vast and beautiful and full of possibilities).

In a nutshell, the movie is about how nobody really cares when Native American women go missing—which is a real, shocking, and devastating thing. The movie succeeds mightily at caring about this and also getting you (the audience) to care about it as well. It does this by showing you in stark, un-retouched detail how bleak and scary and vulnerable life is for these women. I'll come clean in admitting that, at times, this wasn't necessarily a thing I wanted to view on the screen. It was hard to watch.

The film is "great" if by "great" we mean a film with beautiful cinematography that is not only visually stunning but also coheres with what we're supposed to get out of the film. This is added-to by a great Renner performance. Renner, we decided, is not handsome but is super interesting to look at. He's entered the "thoughtful movie" phase of his career in which he will get older and more grizzled and will start doing more movies that look like this, and fewer movies that look like *Mission Impossible*. In general, this is a good development. For what it's worth, my favorite Renner performance is still opposite

Ben Affleck in *The Town*. He plays a great dirtbag.

Wind River, then, sort of follows the art-action-drama paradigm, if such paradigm looks something like this: a.) desolate landscape portraying the depths of human depravity, b.) a rape scene that is so difficult to watch that it almost makes you want to turn the movie off, c.) romantic subtext that is so thinly veiled as to almost not be there at all, d.) ultra-sad drug abuse, e.) an action-movie revenge arc that is almost satisfying but leaves the audience with the feeling that nothing has really been resolved. Not really resolving anything is a staple of the semi-art/semi-action genre, in which signals are mixed by the image of Jeremy Renner with a shotgun on the movie poster (traditional action!) but also the presence of Real Issues.

On Renner and sound: another arty thing is to take a guy who is really good at acting and talking (like Renner, or like Leo DiCaprio in *The Revenant*) and then just have him grunt or mumble a whole bunch. The subtext there is that this guy is such a tormented "man of the earth" that he can scarcely be bothered with saying words . . . but still, I'd like to hear the words.

The Real Issues issue is what keeps this from being a Saturday Night movie. A Saturday Night movie is one you want to watch with a friend or loved one because you have the innate sense that watching movies is supposed to be fun. It's the impulse that makes you purchase a movie because you know you'll watch it again because it makes you feel good. *Wind River* is not a Saturday Night movie.

It's a weeknight and maybe even a watch-it-alone weeknight movie—and not just because it deals with Real Issues. An example of a Real Issues movie that is also a

Saturday Night movie is *Legends of the Fall*. Even though much of the content is dark, there is a redemptive thread. *Wind River* decidedly lacked the all-important redemptive thread. Yes, in the particular case of the movie, "justice" (albeit one man's version) happened and that was, in a way, satisfying. However, there was no sense that anything about life in desolate, rural Wyoming would be any different and there was the sense that the people who could "take" would continue to do so. This may be Taylor Sheridan's wheelhouse, as *Sicario* was the same way.

In this, it was not unlike watching a slice of real life—beautifully rendered yet not especially pleasant.

PART III: SPORTS

Suiting Up with My Son:
Vintage American Football

Originally Published in *The Jackson Sun*

In the third quarter of a game against the Moline Universal Tractors I trudged back to the huddle, covered in sweat and dirt, with my head throbbing from an elbow I took to the jaw a few plays before. I looked to the left in the huddle and my oldest son, Tristan, nodded and gave me a thumbs-up.

"You good, bud?" I asked between gulps of air.

He was great and I knew it because of the smile that was plastered on his face from ear to ear. He had been flying around the field, throwing blocks, returning kicks and looking great in his uniform—doing all the things I used to do when I was young and I mattered as a football player. In a scene right out of a recurring dream, we were teammates on the Rock Island (Illinois) Independents, sweating and bleeding on the same field.

But the thing is, the Rock Island Independents actually played the Moline Universal Tractors in 1920 in the National Football League's first recorded game, back when teams were concentrated in the blue-collar Midwest and traveled to face each other by train. Back when players played for hundreds of dollars instead of millions, had day jobs, and wore long-sleeved wool jerseys and leather helmets.

Several years ago I joined a historical society called the Pro Football Researchers Association and found a small group of (mostly older) people who were as crazy about

football history as I am. I am currently a subscriber to only one magazine—the PFRA's *Coffin Corner Newsletter*—and I tear into it like an excited toddler each time it shows up in my mailbox.

It was through the PFRA that I met Simon Herrera—a software developer from Nashville whose dreams were as grandiose (and probably insane) as my own. "See baby, there are people out there who are sicker than me," I said to my wife.

"You can play, but I want a flapper dress and a cloche hat," she said. That was easy.

Herrera stages authentic, vintage, leather helmet football games as a way to respect and celebrate the history of a league that has grown to billion-dollar multi-national proportions and isn't quite as fun as it was when we were kids.

We met in Nashville.

Herrera showed me the leather helmet, the bright green Rock Island jersey, and the large melon-shaped 1920 football. He thought he hooked me that afternoon, but I was actually all-in the moment I heard about his games.

Each October, Herrera and his partner in football history, Chris Zimmerman, host a Vintage American Football game in Rock Island, Illinois, to commemorate the birthplace of the NFL. The game features era-specific uniforms, rules, officials, and equipment, and is witnessed by old men playing 1920s jazz and women in flapper dresses, easily making it the most charming thing I've ever experienced in football.

Players have a variety of motives. Most are pro football historians, some are local competition-junkies, and a few are ringers whose college football careers ended a year or so ago and are brought in to help their respective teams win because no matter how miniscule the "stakes," any time there are guys competing on a field of any kind, both sides desperately want to win.

But as much as I love football history, I played for one reason only: to suit up with my son. He's in high school and what once seemed like it would take forever—his childhood—is slipping like sand through the hourglass. Moments like these are precious, and I'm grateful to Herrera and Zimmerman for making it happen.

Final Fantasy (or, Reclaiming Sunday Afternoon)

For the first time in more than a decade, I'm not playing fantasy football.

Fantasy football, for the uninitiated, is an online game in which players pick players on NFL teams to populate their own (fantasy) teams and then score points when the NFL players score points in real life. There are entire magazines devoted to fantasy football, along with thousands of websites. I used to provide content for one of these websites. It was the longest autumn of my life—an autumn filled with injury reports, yards per carry averages, and waiver-wire recommendations. I thought it would never end.

Since I have played real football nearly every year of my life, I always felt a little nerdy and ridiculous for playing fantasy football. Until I learned that nearly every able-bodied, red-blooded American male between the ages of 15 and 95 plays it too.

Fantasy football has ruined many a Sunday afternoon for me. I have stood in church, hoping that the sermon would be short so that I could run home and sign Chester Taylor, having heard that Matt Forte tweaked a groin in Saturday's walk-through practice. Before fantasy football I would have given nary a thought to Matt Forte or his groin. I have agonized through victories by my favorite teams (Bears, Colts) because fantasy players on those particular teams have underperformed. I have effectively rooted against favorite teams because I had fantasy players on opposing teams.

I have struggled to find the actual game on the television screen because of all of the scrolling real-time statistics deemed "necessary" by fantasy football. Between the game clock, the scrolling fantasy stats, the promotion for next week's games, and the Fox Sports robots, the game has become the inconsequential thing occupying a few square inches in the middle of the screen. Fantasy has screwed up the aesthetic of televised football, which you could argue screwed up the aesthetic of real, in-person football.

I have one thing to say to fantasy football: I hate you. I hate you for ruining a handful of Sundays each year. I'd like to say that you deepened friendships with the people in my leagues, etc. but that would be a lie. I'd like to say that I enjoyed the championships I won playing fantasy football, but in fact they made me feel sheepish and a little ridiculous about the level of time and effort they took. I'll never again say the words "fantasy research" to my wife when she asks why there's a $9 magazine with a picture of Tom Brady on the cover in our shopping cart at the grocery store. What's more, I'll never again have to utter the words "Tom Brady" and "fantasy" in the same sentence again, and then feel sheepish for uttering those words together.

So this season I'm kicking it on the old-school tip. I'm going to watch football as God intended—without caring about fantasy stats or quietly seething with resentment toward my friend's fantasy football glory. I'm going to stop sketching potential trade scenarios on the bulletin at church. I'm going to re-acquaint myself with my old teams. I'm going to stop talking about my fantasy team to my wife, who never cared anyway, and was always very gracious about not laughing when I brought up my "fantasy team."

I feel like Jerry Maguire in the "Who's coming with me?" scene, where he quits SMI. I know that nobody's coming with me. Not even the Dorothy Boyd character, or the fish ("These fish have manners—the fish are coming with me."). I know that you are probably the Bob Sugar character in this scenario—eating a sandwich and waving at me derisively as I go.

But, like Jerry, I ate two slices of bad pizza, went to bed and grew a football conscience. And like a true young, Reformed, pseudo-theologian, I'm ready to Reclaim Football. Reclaim Sunday afternoon.

Who's coming with me?

Love and Football:
The Lane College Experience

I am a lifelong football addict, and like all addicts I like my fixes to come in a particular way. I've played and coached the sport my entire life and, as such, I have an almost physical ache for it each fall. Ideally I'm playing it, but in lieu of that I'm at least watching a lot—ideally, in person.

When I learned that I'd be teaching at a football-less university in Jackson, TN, I immediately started scoping out the college football in the area and found that . . . there isn't much. The University of Tennessee at Knoxville is six hours away. Memphis is an hour and tickets are expensive. But then I learned that there is a college with football—Lane College—right in my city, and very nearly in my backyard.

My first weekend here I drove through Lane's campus and found it fascinating—old, stately buildings in an older part of town. I drove by their practice field and was disappointed that there were no players on it. I wanted to watch a practice and just be near it (like I said, a sickness). Lane is an HBCU (stands for Historically Black Colleges and Universities) and has an interesting history with my school. When a couple of my best journalism students said, "We should start a journalism partnership with Lane," I enthusiastically agreed—for reasons both philosophical and, admittedly, selfish. Lane has something that I want and that something is college football. A civil-rights hero I am not.

The partnership has been everything that I'd hoped it

would be—fun, stimulating, enriching and redemptive for students and faculty on both sides. It's early, and nothing is ever perfect, but I'm hopeful. Today was Lane's first home football game. They play on a retro high school field here in Jackson whose defining characteristic is a set of very crooked goalposts. The stands are brick, and old. Paint peels. Grass yellows in the bright sun. Rap music throbs out of portable speakers but soon gives way to drumlines and the best marching band music I have ever heard in my entire life.

On my way in, a Lane College professor greeted me with a warm hug. Another offered me barbecue, on the house. I met Lane's president who was warm and hospitable. The game opened with a very evangelical prayer in which both teams, both bands, and both sets of fans bowed heads and prayed for goodwill and harmony between the schools. In all my years of football I've never seen anything like it. My son Maxim and I sat on the front row, just a few feet away from the Lane bench. And though the game was hard and violent—like all good football games are hard and violent—it had zero fights and almost no profanity. At no point did I have to cover my son Maxim's ears, as I've had to do so many times at Spartan Stadium, Ford Field, and many of the other venues we've frequented over the years, where buffoonery is the norm.

Today we played Tuskegee and their white jerseys were emblazoned with the word 'Skeegee (note: I'm an avid jersey collector and want one . . . bad). Their players, like ours, danced to the marching band music during warm-ups. Swagger was present in droves, but it was an unselfconscious kind of redemptive swag. I stood along a fence and noticed a young boy, about my son's age, with his eyes closed and head swaying, dancing (as they say) like nobody was watching. A lone Tuskegee player knelt and prayed in the end zone before the game.

The football wasn't perfect—far from it, in fact. There were, I think, six turnovers in the first nine minutes. Both teams ran the spread offense (no fullbacks, lots of bubble-screens), which I hate. Lane lost 40-14, but it didn't matter. It was a beautiful day of live college football with a team I'm now calling my own. I will be back the very next time they play at home and each time thereafter. Both bands played back and forth at one another, battle style, the entire afternoon. "I could listen to this music all day long," I told my son.

He looked at me like I was crazy and started climbing the fence like he owned the place, and like there was never even a moment of weirdness or division between black and white in Jackson, Tennessee.

Infinite Jest: On Competition and the Joy of Watching Middle-School Tennis

Originally Published in *The Jackson Sun*

The most jarring thing about it is the silence—broken only by occasional laughter and the sound of packs of middle school kids chattering as they walk by.

"This is way more relaxing than football," I texted to my wife, as I sat in the grass, in the sunshine, in front of an open copy of David Foster Wallace's *Infinite Jest* which is about (in part) tennis. I would glance up occasionally to see my son hit a ball and then keep score by placing a tennis ball in this little peg thing that is designed to hold tennis balls—the design of which (the peg/ball thing) struck me as brilliant in its simplicity.

I grew up in a hyper-aggressive football culture and had the chance to eventually play and coach the game at a pretty high level. In this culture the opponent was your "enemy" and you went to "war" on Friday night. In football culture you kept a "chip on your shoulder" and "played angry" and "got after somebody." This was a culture where, after a defeat, it was a requirement to not smile and not laugh, and if there was a bus ride involved it was necessary to just stare out the window glumly, full of regret about how you didn't "leave it all on the field of battle."

Football was something you survived. I have enduring memories of two-a-days . . . bent over at the waist, sucking in gulps of air and trying not to vomit up breakfast, or sitting on a concrete cleat-house floor with my body covered in bruises and open wounds, just staring blankly into space because all I had the energy to do was stare blankly into space. Don't get me wrong, this was cool—it was cool to be a survivor—but it also, quantifiably, really sucked.

I was always anxious and paranoid because I was afraid of losing and afraid of being embarrassed at a "war" that I felt meant way more than it actually did. I was, truth be told, afraid of getting hurt, which in football culture was a thing that you could never admit or talk about out loud. We listened to heavy metal or rap before football games because we were trying to prepare, mentally, to go and do a really counterintuitive thing—fight like men.

Here, at tennis, there is no rap, no metal, and no yelling. The coaches never raise their voices and, in fact, I can't even really tell who the coaches are because nobody is pacing around and frowning and looking miserable. It's never really clear who the winners and losers are. There is no loudspeaker and no announcer praising the winner and shaming the loser.

"Are they playing yet or just warming up?" I ask the dad next to me. He is, as it turns out, the dad of my son's opponent. This is something that would never happen in football—opposing parents hanging out together. We laugh about how neither of us know anything about tennis, and about how he took up tennis in college as a shameless ploy to meet girls.

"Because I don't know anything about this I can't ruin it for him," I explain to the other dad. He laughs because he knows exactly what I'm talking about.

I'm not anti-football. I think there's still a place for football, and toughness, in our culture. In fact, I still love it in the way that you still have affection for a really compelling lover who keeps hurting you but to whom you keep crawling back.

After football games, my parents' home was a triage ward. Bags of ice were dispensed and wounds were cleaned and wrapped. After tennis, my son just tosses his bag in the car and starts chattering—high on victory and a fun afternoon with friends. I will always miss football, but this is really nice too.

Could Arena Football Provide the Answer to America's Football Problem?

Originally Published in *The Jackson Sun*

I am a college professor who very occasionally moonlights as an arena football player. These two worlds couldn't be more different, but here is one interesting point of overlap: as one of my sorority-girl students told me, "It's all about the pictures."

What she meant was that her sorority formal was an exercise in masterminding lighting, camera angles, and wardrobe to emerge from the evening with the perfect picture to prove that the evening (and, at some level, she herself) existed. This became real to me in a bathroom about an hour before game time at an indoor sports arena in Maryland, where I took a furtive selfie in the uniform of my team-for-a-night—the New England Bobcats. I am more than a little ashamed of this (the bathroom selfie). It feels good to talk about it.

The Bobcats are a first-year team in the Elite Indoor Football League, and are owned by Cynthia Hudson who couldn't be warmer, friendlier, or more accommodating, and who sounds just like "Irish" Micky Ward's mom in *The Fighter* (2010, Mark Wahlberg). Hudson is professional indoor football's only female owner and, judging by the quality of her coaching staff, players and uniforms, has put together a first-rate organization.

Arena football is an addiction for me that started in 2006 when I was a member of the Battle Creek (MI) Crunch and really sucked. Since then, I've been on a mission to perfect my craft and suck a little less each time. In this pursuit I am not only battling Father Time (who never loses), but also the realities of a career, several side-hustles, injuries, family life (I'm trying to be a good husband and father, often failing) and the very real and niggling concern that doing this is really unwise for a guy my age.

Last weekend the Bobcats opened their season against the Western Maryland Warriors in Frederick, Maryland. Here are a few things about this experience that I loved, and that could in some way (stay with me) provide answers to America's football crisis, which can be summed up by the phrases "head injuries" and "divisive social issues."

- My doctorate-holding best friend from college using his "outside voice" to explain the abolitionist movement (we drove through Harpers Ferry) to my wife, in an arena full of black guys. One of the best parts of these football experiences is always being in the distinct racial minority but *always* having it work out in great and interesting ways. While the media insisted last season on highlighting the NFL's cultural and racial differences, I am always charmed by how the game brings people together.

- The usual fascinating mix of ritualized, shouted swearing juxtaposed against the fact that we recite The Lord's Prayer a bunch of times. This never gets old for me.

- Hearing the following, pre-game, about the referees: "The refs are running late and have someplace to be afterward . . . so expect a quick game."

- A variety of truly great, talented players with college pedigrees who have slipped through conventional scouting's cracks: linebacker Ruben Encarnacion, defensive back Alex Hulme, and quarterback Najee Hillman stood out, but I could have listed several more. Actually, I will: running back Darryl Cyprien and 6'9" tackle and former two-sport college athlete Terrell Correia played exceptional games as well.

- Regarding head injuries: in the arena game (8 on 8, 50-yard field), there is no downhill running game, no pulling or trapping on the offensive line, and very few "in-breaking" pass patterns, meaning that while the game is still violent and exciting there seem to be far fewer catastrophic head injuries. I'm not a doctor, but this is just something I've observed. It's hard to get up a full head of steam on a field that short and narrow, which mitigates against head-rattling "kill shots."

- I may have broken my right thumb (the all-important "space bar" thumb for a writer) but the experience was still absolutely worth it.

- I may or may not have thought one of my coaches was having a stroke, slumped up against and arena wall in a corner during the game, and went to check on him only to discover that he may or may not have been sneakily peeing into an empty Gatorade bottle. The football world, while violent and intense, is always very predictably funny in ways that keep me coming back.

I was supposed to be there to long-snap, only to find that the arena we were in didn't have goalposts, so I got in several reps as a nose tackle thanks to some gracious rotation work by defensive coordinator Mark Stevens, who along with head coach Bill Savary, is a truly great guy.

These guys probably have no idea what a blessing it was for me to be able to do this—to enjoy a sore but beautiful drive home with my wife the following day, reflecting on the joys of being a competitive football player, just one more time. As the shameful bathroom selfie attests, this league exists, the New England Bobcats exist, and I existed as an athlete again . . . if only for a night. For that I am grateful.

Sports and Moral Superiority

A friend of mine shot me an article this morning—his response to a PhD-type (not a PhD type, but an actual PhD) arguing that football is morally objectionable because it is intrinsically violent. The PhD argues for baseball as a morally superior sport (Clemens, McGwire, et al were unavailable for comment, apparently).

Caveat Time: I don't know why I feel compelled to defend football in situations like these, but that's exactly what I'm going to do . . . probably because I've spent my whole life either playing or coaching it. Really, I should be busy pulling my hair out about John Piper interviewing Rick Warren, or something that really "matters" (actually, kidding aside, I'm thinking I might pull my hair out about that tomorrow).

My qualifications: None, really (see: above).

Douglas Groothuis (the academic) makes some valid points. I'll be the first to admit that football is *hella-violent*. I've played it a bunch and I've also boxed, and I can tell you (opinion here, of course) that it's way more violent that boxing. It's controlled chaos. That's also what makes it almost ridiculously addictive. Not saying that all addictive things are good (of course) but I think there may be something to the idea that it is partly the violence and atmosphere of danger that make it compelling to people. Television ratings and league revenues of late would suggest that football is more compelling to people than baseball.

Groothuis argues that baseball is "intellectually superior to football." This was the most laughable one to me. Any high school football player (not to mention college or professional) who has ever had to memorize a textbook-thick playbook and a myriad of assignments on a football field will tell you that it takes a ton of brainpower—it's also no small feat to execute said assignments while feeling the effects of fatigue and the violent collisions that make football, football. Still, I have a great deal of respect for baseball, strategically. Saying that one sport is "superior" from a strategic perspective is like saying that David Foster Wallace is "smarter" than Albert Einstein. They're both geniuses. Let's face facts: It's ridiculously hard to excel (on a world class level) at any sport, and on a high level there is a great deal of strategy inherent in nearly every team sport.

Also, the fact that I've interviewed professional baseball players as a part of my past job as a sports journalist was proof to me that major league baseball players were amongst the least compelling human beings I've ever met in any walk of life. I've had better, richer conversations with the students in my son's second-grade public school classroom. For that matter I've had better conversations with pets.

Aside: Best Interviews, by Sport:
- Boxing (ultra-violent)
- Any women's sport (good interviews, girls)
- Hockey (semi-violent)
- NBA basketball
- Football
- And bringing up the rear is that bastion of moral and intellectual superiority, baseball.

Also: If baseball is so morally and intellectual superior, why don't its heroes reflect some of that? Given its supposed inherent virtue, it would follow that many professional baseball players be thoughtful, reflective, clean-living, and semi-intellectual. While this is probably true for some in the sport, it's certainly not the norm. I don't think Mickey Mantle was reading Martin Heidegger in those hotel rooms on the road.

Here's the thing: both sports are chock full of super-seedy people (see: Total Depravity). You could go to any midwestern hotel ballroom and find an insurance seminar full of super-seedy people there too (see again: Depravity). The list of derelicts, drug-addicts and cheaters in baseball is as long as the list of the same in football. Both sports, as well, are full of whatever Groothuis (or I) would call "good" people (meaning, probably, the kinds of people we'd be comfortable hanging around with which doesn't necessarily make them "good").

As part of his argument for baseball's superiority "as a cultural form" (more on that later), Groothuis explains that "intellectuals have been drawn to write and reflect" on baseball. They (Mailer, Plimpton, Hemingway, et al) did the same thing with boxing—a sport which Groothuis probably wouldn't bother dirtying his cap/gown with vis-à-vis it being or not being a "cultural form."

That being said, I'm pretty sure athletes, coaches, fans, and owners aren't bothering with Groothuis or the Evangelical Philosophical Society either—a street (not bothering) which runs, and has always run, both ways. The point being that nobody cares about baseball or football as "cultural forms." We care about those sports because of the people they allow us to meet (teammates, lifelong friends) and the experiences they allow us to have (freshly cut grass, time with fathers, catch, stadium dogs, stadium beers, trading cards, and even injuries/rehabbing injuries) or because they allow us to make money (if we're in the business at some level). Baseball and football will be around as long as people want to watch/play them . . . and no amount of white-papering is really going to make any difference.

I have absolutely no problem with somebody liking baseball more than football. I love baseball too. What's weird to me is the need to spiritualize-slash-infuse-with-spiritual-slash-moral-qualities things that are probably just morally kind of neutral outside of the individual people doing the playing/coaching/watching.

So what difference does any of this make? Probably none. As far as Christians in sports, Timmy Tebow and his lantern jaw, famous evangelical parents, and underwear commercials are garnering more mainstream thought-space and attention than a lifetime's worth of any Doug Groothuis and Ted Kluck projects ever will. But what's interesting about this, to me, is that thinky Christians are definitely levelling their thought-guns on football of late. It'll be interesting to see where it all goes from here (probably nowhere).

Deconstructing NFL Uniforms

Originally Published in *The Jackson Sun*

As I type this, I'm anticipating a Monday Night Football matchup between the Atlanta Falcons and the Seattle Seahawks. In 1987 (red/black Falcons with the Ohio State pants) or 1993 (black/gray Falcons), this would have been an aesthetically pleasing contest featuring interesting colors and designs. Tonight, it might be the grossest matchup in NFL history from a uniform standpoint, as Atlanta's current mess of a uniform features an early-2000s Arena Football League design aesthetic, and Seattle is currently wearing a shade of blue that doesn't actually exist in real life. I'll watch the game because I love football, but that's the only reason.

In 1987 or 1993 teams had the freedom to choose their own uniform manufacturers, which resulted in a delightful mix of fabrics, fonts, and cuts. Today, teams are all clad in the same Nike sausage-casings and we miss the nuance of Durene fabric ('80s-'90s Steelers) and porthole-mesh ('80s-'90s Seahawks) while the uniformity (as it were) is emblematic of the beige-ness of the NFL product in general.

Anyway, here's a Worst-to-Best ranking of NFL uniforms . . .

The "Made More Terrible" Because They Used to be Awesome Tier

Atlanta Falcons: Hard to look at. Pick any other era of Falcons football and it's better than the uniform purgatory we're in currently.

Washington Redskins: I like maroon. I like gold. Maroon and gold are gross together. Reference the 1980s Joe Gibbs Redskins for a master's class on how to handle maroon and gold. The Gibbs era squad wore the maroon jersey with a basic white pant accented by two simple stripes up the side. Done.

Seattle Seahawks: In the '80s the Seahawks were uniform *innovators*, utilizing both a huge number font and porthole mesh back when nobody was doing it. Today the uniform looks like it should be worn by a discarded third-tier Marvel Universe character.

Tampa Bay Buccaneers: The current Bucs uniform is hard to watch. The orange-creamsicle original was sublimely wonderful. The pewter-power era was somewhere in between.

Arizona Cardinals: A *great* color scheme ruined by over-creativity in the early 2000s. This uniform stinks in part because the old one was so simple and great.

Denver Broncos: See, exactly what I wrote about the Cardinals. The Broncos had an *amazing*, natural branding moment, The Orange Crush, made possible by their orange jerseys. And then they switched to a boring blue jersey with arena football accents.

The "It Just Sucks and Was Never Good" Tier

Cincinnati Bengals: A mess. Moreso now than ever. This uniform fails to look good against *any* opponent.

Tennessee Titans: Meh.

Baltimore Ravens: This has always been a hard-to-look-at uniform. Didn't the late-'90s Colorado Rockies teach us that purple and black together is just a bad idea?

The Teams That Are Due for a Design Change Tier

Carolina Panthers: Still rocking a sad mid-'90s black-teal combo with essentially the same boring design scheme.

Houston Texans: When the Texans launched their franchise they were bad, as all expansion teams are. They're still bad, and they're still wearing the same uniform. At least they have DeShaun Watson.

New England Patriots: It's not bad . . . but it's not great, like the '70s/'80s Pats uni. The logo on the helmet is completely forgettable.

Philadelphia Eagles: It doesn't exactly suck, but the dark green with black accents screams early-2000s. Anyone else up for a return to the Kelly green Randall Cunningham-era uni?

The "No-Expectations/Pleasantly Surprised" Tier

Jacksonville Jaguars: Neither the city nor the team have any cultural tradition to speak of, so the Jags uniform each year is kind of an adventure. But not a bad one.

Miami Dolphins: Okay, but forgettable. The all-whites look like a child's pajamas.

New Orleans Saints: A better than average NFL uniform. But the huge, gold collar is a mistake.

The "Indefensible Design Changes" Tier

Cleveland Browns: The Browns had one of the cleanest, most iconic uniforms in professional sports. The brown jersey with the white pant was a delight. Words on pants? Not necessary.

Minnesota Vikings: A textbook case of being too creative. What was wrong with the Randy Moss version? Or the Tommy Kramer version, for that matter?

Detroit Lions: Notwithstanding the early-2000s black-accented disaster, pick almost any era of the Detroit Lions uniform and it's better than the current one. Sometimes more creativity isn't better.

The Almost-Vintage Almost-Great Tier

San Francisco 49ers: Prisoners of a "meh" color-scheme, kudos to the 'Niners for settling on the best version of their uniform.

Buffalo Bills: The Bills have done a great thing by harkening back to their greatest uniform era (white helmet, blue jersey).

Los Angeles/San Diego Chargers: It's almost the 1960s Chargers uniform, and the jersey is reminiscent of the great Dan Fouts-era version. But somehow it manages to be neither, and in doing so manages to not be great.

Los Angeles Rams: The only Ram uniform that has never looked great is the Kurt Warner-era version. Unfortunately, they still wear it sometimes.

New York Jets: It's a very watchable, clean uniform, although I think the '80s/big-number/thick-stripe Jets uni was more distinctive.

Kansas City Chiefs: Clean and easy to look at. The Schottenheimer-era uni was the best . . . but this one is solid too.

New York Giants: The Giants have settled on a vintage look that is very pleasing to the eye but falls short of being great.

The Classic and Almost Great Tier

Pittsburgh Steelers: Thank you, Rooney family, for never really tinkering with this uniform.

Green Bay Packers: Thank you, municipally-owned Packers, for never really tinkering with this uniform.

Indianapolis Colts: Clean and simple and oh-so-easy to look at.

Dallas Cowboys: The dark blue jersey with the silver pant is sublime; the white jersey with the silver pant is just very good.

The Classic and Amazing Tier

Oakland Raiders: Silver. Black. Clean. Sublime.

Chicago Bears: This uniform has *always* just looked good. Dark blue, orange, and clean. Plus, Walter Payton wore it.

Sports Will Not Solve Any of Our Problems

The obligatory postgame handshake has to be the most inauthentic, awkward two minutes in American culture. Long upheld by proponents of "character," this basically involves each team lining up, walking past each other, and offering up a limp, lifeless hand to be "shaken" by the opponent (meaning to have the palm of which sort of half-heartedly slapped). Eye contact is rarely made. It's even worse for the coaches, who come at the end of the line and have to actually shake the hand of the rage-a-holic slob across the field who had a 150-pound sixth grader carrying the ball and didn't play any of his subs per the rules. Make no mistake about it, shaking the hand of this guy is no easy thing to do.

Yet, the handshake is supposed to signify the fact that "sportsmanship" has been upheld when in fact the whole time (as a player and as a coach) I have harbored Legarette Blount fantasies of punching the crap out of one of my opponents in one of these handshake lines. In fact, when Blount did that, everyone went nuts about what a thug he was, but I think it might have been one of the most honest things I've ever seen in sports. The other guy probably deserved it and, what's more, it's not like the previous three hours (of football) are exactly an exercise in brotherly love and kindness.

I was reminded of this yesterday at my son's sixth grade football game. My son is a good athlete and a good football player. He plays on a good team with good coaches who know what they're doing and treat the kids very well. There is much to affirm. They win most of the time. But he lost the game to the same collection of thugs he's been barely losing to his entire life. These are the kids who beat him by a half an inch in the long jump in track season or by a half a second on the 100 meter hurdles. These are the kids who routinely drop F-bombs in his face, on the field and on the track. They hit after the whistle. These are kids whose hands are hard to shake. These are the kids whose dads I stare down in the parking lot.

My son's father is not very gracious in these situations. Harkening back to my own football career, and reflecting just in general on how hard life is in a godless, loveless culture, I give my son great advice like "hit him in the earhole" and "if you bring your forearm up into his chin, that will shut him up . . . don't worry, it's legal."

What's sad is that I'm right. The nature of football is that it's a self-regulating culture. The kid who drops F-bombs in your ear will not respect you until you've planted him in the ground and made him hurt. And then, ironically, you might become friends. But not until then. The sad reality is that football is probably the fairest place on earth. It doesn't get any easier in the cubicle or the boardroom, where there's no hope of a hard block or tackle to level the proverbial playing field.

The reality of the matter is that life in real sports is not like life in the Disney version of sports. In the Disney version the good-hearted ragtag bunch bands together and beats the team full of thugs with dark visors on their helmets. In doing so, they perfect the imperfect. They "right" societal wrongs and they give all of us in the audience the hope that there may just be some justice in this dark world. We leave the theater with some renewed hope that the jerk in the office or the bully on the playground might just get his.

Because we're created in God's image, it's normal for us to long after this justice. We want it for the same reason we want to see Rocky beat the cheating, bloodthirsty Ivan Drago. We want to see what we perceive as good triumphing over what we perceive as evil. What's insidious is that we all perceive ourselves as good. Another reality is that I don't "deserve" to win any more than the idiot across the field. We are both capable of nothing good apart from Christ, meaning that my little ragtag bunch of winners is no more deserving than his collection of visor-clad giants who appear to be 16 years old.

In real life, the good-hearted ragtag bunch of kids bands together and still loses by two touchdowns. In real life, sports will not solve any of our problems, and it's foolish of us to think they can. Yet I still think it, every week. In real life I still think this is the year that the track dad with the whistle and stopwatch around his neck will get his comeuppance, courtesy of my son and the rest of his team.

In real life the kid with the obnoxious, insufferably-arrogant jerk of a dad might just go to the NFL. I know because I've met this kid and his dad in the NFL more than once. I'm reminded that the NFL is not eternity. The NFL is not the destination that will solve anyone's problems, as the last few weeks have painfully illustrated. The Bible doesn't say, "I press on toward the prize for which God has called me . . . to the NFL." Though in many cases this is how we treat it—even as Christians. We treat winning and money and professional sports as the "blessings" that trump all other blessings. We treat these things as though they are the tangible proof that God is working and that he loves us.

The truth is, God loves us so much that he won't allow these petty, light, and momentary things to make me feel, even for a moment, like I am God myself. Because if I'm righting all of my perceived societal wrongs on the field, myself, I have no need for the God of the universe (in that moment). I go home one step closer to being the smug, self-satisfied, and insufferably arrogant jerk of a dad whose company I go to great lengths to avoid.

And my son (age 12), for all of his competitiveness, is not a mercenary fighting on my behalf. He is a kid who still occasionally plays with stuffed animals and loves reading *Calvin and Hobbes*, even though for a few hours each weekend he plays a grown man's game. And I love him, no matter what.

Doug Drabek, the Jackson Generals, and Nostalgia

Originally Published in *The Jackson Sun*

When I first encountered Jackson Generals pitching coach Doug Drabek last night at the ballpark, he was drinking a cup of coffee in spite of the fact that it was, by my rough estimate, 150 degrees out, with ninety-four percent humidity. Drabek is someone who doesn't mess around when it comes to caffeinating.

Because I subconsciously live most of my life for nostalgia—I have very little use for the present or the future—Drabek was far and away the best thing about a great night at the ballpark with my son Maxim. Not that we interacted at all. At my age it's not about interacting, and actually interacting might ruin it. It was just Drabek's presence, which made me think of his incredible hair-slash-mustache situation in the '80s (take a minute to Google-image this), which made me think of multi-use stadiums with AstroTurf, which made me think of those Pirates teams that were so much fun to watch.

This resulted in texts to my buddies, one of whom recounted the following story: "When I was in ninth grade I babysat for some kids who had ESPN and I watched Drabek come within one out of a no-hitter." In the grand scheme of my life and my friend's life, the no-hitter is relatively meaningless—actually completely meaningless, except as a conduit to a fun conversation in the midst of a fun night at the ballpark. Which means that maybe it is the opposite of meaningless? If seeing Drabek is an excuse to text my buddy, which results in a genuinely great conversation, perhaps his life and his vocation are the opposite of meaningless?

I thought a lot about vocation while watching Drabek wing wild pitches at the starting catcher in the bullpen before the game. It is an act that he has probably performed hundreds of nights each year, in hundreds of hot, unglamorous stadiums in the Southern League and points below—all of this after a Cy Young-winning career, plying his trade in the biggest, best, loudest stadiums in the world for over a decade.

Drabek is a baseball lifer and was far and away the most famous, accomplished, impressive person in the entire ballpark last night. However, in the 5-6 minutes I spent semi-creepily watching him in the bullpen, he seemed to get most excited about arriving at the park early the next day so he could take a turn on the impressive riding mower the groundskeepers use. This is what work looks like—basically a slow, monotonous grind in the same direction.

I think my students could learn a lot from Drabek, as I learned a lot from watching him. I am mid-career. In a sense my career kind of looks like Drabek's in that I published most of my impressive books in my early 30s, and now I'm teaching—which, like being a minor-league pitching coach, involves doing the same stuff every day (and every year) with young people, all of whom eventually move on (which is hard).

Also like Drabek, I'm not sure I dream of the "big time" anymore. I don't know him (actually, update to what I wrote above: it *would* be cool to meet him), but I'm guessing he doesn't sit there in the bullpen in Jackson and

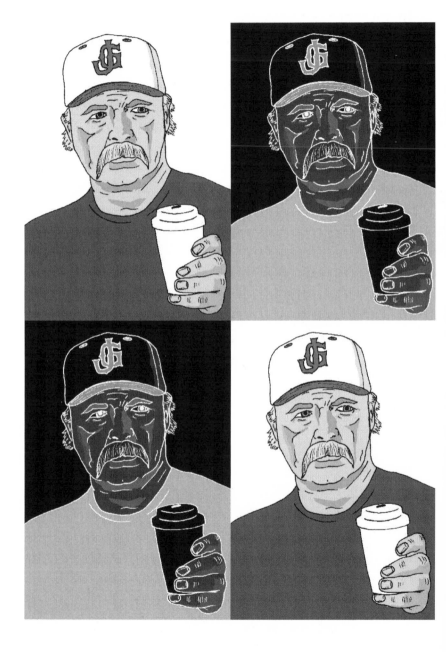

dream about sitting in a bullpen in Fenway Park or Wrigley Field. Your mind just doesn't work that way when you're mid-career. It seems dumb to do that. Rather, I hope he enjoys the work somewhat, and enjoys each day for what it brings. The thing of it is, the baseball grind at the AA level is ultra-respectable, which is what I'd like my students to see. It's far cooler to warm up a catcher in a AA bullpen than it is to take selfies and dream of fame.

I distinctly remember going to a minor league baseball game in Fort Wayne, IN with my dad in which he got all nostalgic and excited about seeing Don Zimmer (old baseball legend, dad's generation) in the dugout. Last night I had the same experience with Drabek and my son. If baseball exists only to deliver these moments, then it is the very definition of meaningful.

Why Sports Fandom?

This is a question I ask myself when I am seething with rage and exasperating my wife at a youth football game. It's a question a pastor friend—who is a fellow Syracuse University football fan—asked me after the Orange lost to Maryland recently. "Is there anything even remotely redeeming and pleasing to the Lord about this?" he asked, semi-rhetorically . . . and then we talked about it for an hour because that's what we do. The "this" he was referring to was his own "seething with rage and exasperating his wife" moment after the Orange game.

On the surface there doesn't seem to be much that's redeeming about being in a bad mood after the team which you don't play on, don't coach, and otherwise have nothing to do with loses a football game that takes place two hundred miles away from your home. In fact, it's embarrassing and the kind of thing we end up apologizing to our wives about later.

"When I see the orange and blue on the field, I see my childhood," he explains. "I'm a fan of the teams I favor because of what I love. "The team" represents people, places, principles, and practices that I'm devoted to. The team holds my devotion, so the team holds me."

Sports fandom doesn't make sense at all to people who don't care about sports, in much the same way that I don't care about musical theater (for example). I wouldn't cross the street to see a musical in the same way that, apart from me, my wife would never-ever choose to watch a football game. That said, I still want her to understand it, and I want to understand it better myself. This is why we take the time to write about it and think about it.

Our Rooting Interests Are a Reflection of Our Values

I explain to my friend that there's something cool about his decision to support the Pittsburgh Pirates and the Syracuse Orange football program (which is of course a very different animal than supporting the Syracuse Orange basketball program). In the same way that he pours himself out, completely anonymously, as the pastor of a small, needy congregation in a small town, he is similarly pouring himself out on behalf of teams that are under-the-radar and far from perfect. This brings its own particular kind of joy.

The guy who gets his MDiv and immediately looks for one of the twenty-five pastoral jobs at the local rich, thriving megachurch is probably the same kind of guy who roots for the New York Yankees. This is a low-risk, low-reward proposition. Being the "Pastor of Young Adults Whose Names Start with the Letters A through D" isn't in and of itself bad, nor is cheering for the Yankees. It's just different than cheering for a team that you perceive as needing you in some way (which is, in itself, completely irrational, but I'll get there).

"A part of me still craves being with the big shots so that I can get attention," Cory writes. "Yet I've learned to love being with the ones who don't get attention. Even more I love seeing others love them.

"A reason that I don't watch the Steelers with the rigor that I watch the football Orange is that the Steelers get plenty of attention, so mine is superfluous. But the Orange need me. They don't get respect—including from their own sometime fans—so they need what I can give them."

We Root for Who Our Dads Rooted For

"I love my dad," Cory writes. "I have to start here, because I wouldn't care about sports without my dad. As a child I liked sports in theory but struggled with uncoordination, excessive orderliness, fear of looking stupid and of getting hurt, and preference for the mind over the body. But my dad doggedly taught me to play and thence enjoy sports, ushering me into a world I never would have known—or shared with him—otherwise."

My dad did too. My best sports memories all include him. This is all-encompassing and has less to do with fandom and more to do with just being with him. We went to games together (Indianapolis Colts, Indiana University, Ball State, Taylor, and Blackford High School). We lifted weights and threw routes together, training for my promising high school football career. We pushed my pickup truck up and down the street together, training for my abject failure of a college football career. This might sound crazy to most people, but for us it was Nirvana. Dad grew up in Chicago, so I was—and am—a Bears fan.

"Dad grew up in central Pennsylvania and was unswervingly loyal to the Pittsburgh Pirates and Steelers," Cory writes. "Oddly, Dad wasn't loyal to Penn State. So when we moved to a suburb of Syracuse when I was seven he easily slid into rooting for the football and basketball Orangemen. Naturally, so did I. When I see my four teams—Pirates, Steelers, Orange football and men's basketball—I see my dad and the hours we've talked about them together."

We love perfecting what needs it.

"I have a sickness," Cory writes. "It is that I hate dwelling in imperfection and disorder. However, in most cases I hate dwelling in perfection even more, because perfect places strike me as inauthentic, pretentious, and exclusive. Worse, I feel like if I am not perfecting the imperfect then my life is meaningless. So I have to be in the settings that are most likely to drive me crazy. Like I said—sick."

Hence our affinity for Syracuse football. When we talk about the Orange during my morning commutes to teach at the small University whose sports I have no active interest in, we always talk about the team as though it's *our* responsibility to fix it. As though it is our own unique insights that will fix the running game. As though Scott Shafer will somehow intuit our conversations and scrap the spread offense just because I hate watching all of the bubble screens.

"A very strange thing happened to me," Cory writes. "I was living away from Syracuse, and the worse the program got, the more attached to it I became. It was as if the more humiliated the team made me, the more firmly I committed to seeing it straightened out. This was while many fans dealt with the shame by pretending that the program didn't exist.

"Here you need to understand a critical part of my madness. I actually believe that I, who spend almost no money on any of my teams, make them better merely by paying attention to them. This is why I am not entertained by watching recorded sporting events. I have to watch them live, because only if the outcome is not already decided can I help them win by watching them on a television hundreds of miles away. It doesn't matter that I know that this belief is total lunacy—I operate by it anyway."

This is the irrational part—well, one of them. We've both gone all-in on Syracuse football. I chose them because I liked their (then) new hire Doug Marrone. I liked what he represented, which was old-school, smash-mouth running games and a good defense, as well as discipline. I liked that the team was under-the-radar and that if they were to succeed, I would have gotten in on the ground floor. I have completely enjoyed their meteoric rise from absolute ineptitude to minor-bowl mediocrity. It has been a blast.

What's the moral? Or is there one?

"When I love my teams I'm loving myself, because my teams represent and project what my self holds profoundly dearly," Cory writes. "Thus my teams' performance makes me proud of my 'self' or ashamed of it."

This strikes us both as the craziest part of all. The fact that I have an inkling of pride or shame because of what a team does is, at worst, insane and, at best, just really stupid and immature. This is more understandable in a youth-sports context in that at least it's my son out there and, at some level, how he performs could be a reflection on me. Still, it feels crazy.

"The problem," Cory claims, "is that idolatry is the

practice of worshiping my idealized self-projection: the image that I partly am and partly wish I was, in order to replace the dependent image of God in me with an independent image of self. Sports fandom is a very easy way to do that."

When I freak out about my son's pee-wee team's performance (pause to reflect on how sad/shameful that is) I am worshiping my idealized self-projection. I partly am a guy who knows a lot about football. I partly am a guy who has played and coached it semi-well in a lot of different contexts for a lot of years. But perfection—winning all the time and always being great—is what I partly wish I embodied (but fell far short of) as a player.

"However, to the extent that these aspects of myself that are projected in these teams are good and lovingly and providentially shaped by my Creator, because they are also aspects of him, then to cheer for my teams is to reflect his image in me," Cory continues. "So at the moment that I am drawn into my teams' triumphs and woes, how do I know whether I am worshiping the creature (self, as god) or the Creator (God, in self)?"

We don't know, but we think the answer has something to do with love.

Fan-Controlled Professional Football is Real

Originally Published in *The Jackson Sun*

Here are two things that are true:

1. I once co-wrote a satirical rapture novel called *Re: Raptured*, which featured a messianic quarterback who was controlled by an old Sega Genesis controller via a microchip implanted in his neck.

2. I am hopelessly addicted to playing football and even at my advanced age am, at this very moment, talking to several semi – pro and indoor football leagues, casting about for anyone who will let me suit up and play (note to teams: I'm a long snapper and emergency FB/DE). Am I proud of this? Not really. Am I filled with childlike excitement at the idea of suiting up "one more time"? Absolutely.

I recently found a group of "serial tech investors" (their words) who may be able to bring both motifs together seamlessly, for me. In *Die Hard*, Hans Gruber explained that "It's Christmas, Theo, the season of miracles." My miracle may arrive in the form of the Fan Con-trolled Football League.[6]

The Fan Controlled Football League comes along at a very dangerous time for conventional professional football. During the few moments of gameplay in which the National Football League wasn't calling defensive holding

---

[6] https://www.fcfl.io/about-us

or reviewing the "catch rule," it was dealing with a cornucopia of divisive off-field issues that resulted in widespread fan cynicism. Enter the FCFL. Enter a way of thinking about pro football that isn't reverential and pathologically serious.

"The FCFL is about what fans want to do," explained league CEO Sohrob Farudi. Farudi has partnered with former NFL player Ray Austin and a cadre of other tech, entertainment, and sports-industry veterans to provide a fan experience that is part videogame and part live-action pro football "Built on the Blockchain, and backed by FAN token." And for the record, nobody is controlled via a microchip neck implant and Sega controller.

In the FCFL fans draft players, hire and fire coaches, and call plays, all via a mobile app and games that will be uniquely broadcast via Twitch. Per Farudi, the game presentation will have a "videogame feel," given a unique combination of cameras on players, drone shots, and biometrics. The league will feature eight teams, one centralized studio arena, and one-hour games.

"Fans are able to connect on a different level," said Farudi. "They're connecting with the idea that it's *their* team."

Last year the group piloted the idea on one far-flung professional indoor team—the Salt Lake Screaming Eagles. The result was fan engagement from 100 different countries. "We wanted to prove that the tech worked, and wouldn't disrupt the game flow," Farudi explained.

So what does this mean for my own playing endeavors? Farudi graciously extended an opportunity to suit up at an FCFL practice or two later this year—mic'd and camera'd to the hilt—allowing fans a chance to see what a journalist talks and thinks about during football action. "Maybe the fans will rally behind you and vote you into a game," he said.

Maybe. Stay tuned.

On Childhood Heroes

"I can't believe I still have this," said a tearful Brian Bosworth in an ESPN *30 for 30* called "Brian and the Boz."

"This is something I'm not proud of. This is not who I am. And I've apologized to my teammates and my school and my coach because of this."

He is the picture of brokenness and contrition. "If there is one thing I could take back . . . I would take this back. Sometimes it's good to have reminders of the mistakes you make . . . so I'll keep it."

He is speaking of a t-shirt emblazoned with "National Communists Against Athletes" which he famously wore to the 1987 Rose Bowl game—a game from which he was suspended because of a positive steroid test.

For the uninitiated, Brian Bosworth was an All-American linebacker at Oklahoma in the mid-'80s, a lightning-rod for controversy (more below), owner of a fantastic mullet, and perhaps the first and maybe only genuinely cool white athlete in the 1980s. He created an alter-ego called "The Boz" which became his "brand" (before that term was worn out by a generation of uncool business books) and which he used to gather and market to his "tribe" (see: uncool business books, worn-out terms).

I was a member of his tribe. I bought a copy of his "autobiography" (quotes because it was ghostwritten by a pre-fame Rick Reilly, who was really the first Bill Simmons) and read it all on a trip to the University of Wisconsin where I would attend their summer football camp as a mostly-uncool white linebacker trying desperately to

to be like my new hero.

Bosworth was ahead of his time inasmuch as he wasn't okay with the NCAA profiteering from his exploding and very lucrative image while he got nothing. He would have fit right in today, but in 1987 he desecrated the first church of college football. He was never forgiven.

The Boz, today, is known primarily for the mullet, the steroids, getting freight-trained by Bo Jackson and a disappointing NFL career. The sentence that follows will, hopefully, set some of that straight at least for a few readers: The Boz was an exceptionally good inside linebacker. He could run from sideline to sideline, had great instincts and, were it not for injuries, would have had a very successful NFL career. Brian Bosworth, the linebacker, was not a media creation. He was all football player. He was legitimate.

After his lightning-rod career at Oklahoma, Bosworth was selected in the supplemental draft, signed the richest contract (to that point) in the history of the Seahawks franchise, had a great rookie season in 1987 with Seattle and then fizzled shortly thereafter due to injuries. He then embarked on a series of B-grade action movie appearances and, apparently, very little else. He dropped from the public eye as quickly has he put himself into it in the late 1980s.

But that's not what's interesting about the documentary. What's interesting is repentance. There isn't a shred of bravado or "standing on his own rights" left in Bosworth. What remains is a very humble, genuine, and likeable middle-aged man who drank deeply from the fountain of fame and ego and found that it ruined his life.

Now he's trying to explain all of that to his teenage son, who accompanies him on the documentary as they rifle through boxes of Boz-related memorabilia in a Texas storage facility.

This is a portrayal that should be meaningful for us, as Christians, being that true repentance and brokenness are such a part of our experience in Christ. His tears flow freely in this documentary as he shares his sins with his son. It occurs to me that I've never been prouder of a childhood hero.

Some of the film's participants extend forgiveness. Others don't. Some of them understand Bosworth's contrition. Others don't.

"There's more to life than paper clippings, accolades, and rewards," he says, tearfully. He summed up the era best as he was showing a photograph to his son of himself, in sunglasses, on a media day podium surrounded by reporters shoving microphones in his face. "Awesome," said his son.

"You see 'awesome' but I see 'lost,'" the Boz replies. "I'm up here trying to be a deity. But I'm just a football player."

Do I Have to Like Kurt Warner's Hall of Fame Speech, Just Because We're Both Christians?

Originally Published in *The Jackson Sun*

I am a follower of Christ and I also disliked Kurt Warner's Pro Football Hall of Fame speech, which was less a speech and was more a point-by-point 32-minute retelling of the life story of Kurt Warner which (life story, retelling) seemed fascinating and satisfying . . . primarily to Kurt Warner.

Last night I sat for an interview with a large Christian Media Outlet in which I said some positive and negative things about Kurt Warner's speech. A couple of hours later I received a very gracious text from the reporter, explaining that his editor had chosen to omit my negative comments and keep the positive ones, because he didn't want to ruin "Kurt's big moment."

I could have set my watch by this particular response from said Christian Media Outlet, inasmuch as it's not my first rodeo with mainstream Christian media.

This is ironic in that one of the things about the Kurt Warner narrative that Christians relish most is the part where he says positive things about Christ which get cut in the editing room. Christians relish this because it allows us to feel mildly persecuted, which is a thing we enjoy feeling. The irony lies in the fact that when I said something negative about Kurt Warner, that part was left on the cutting room floor as well.

But this begs the question: Just because Kurt Warner and I believe the same things about Christ, the Bible, and eternity, do I have to think that everything he does and says is fabulous? Or am I allowed to think that his speech was fifteen minutes too long (it was, per my own internal clock, and also per the requirements of the Hall of Fame), mechanical (none of the jokes worked as he was obviously reading the whole thing), and tonally self-congratulatory?

I know this sounds like a Christian "going after" another Christian. It's not. I appreciate Warner for his public professions of faith. I did love that he honored his dad, Trent Green, and Christ. These were all really good moments. Additional good Kurt Warner moments include almost all of his moments on the field, where he was a truly great player. But Hall of Fame night felt like Kurt Warner performing *as* Kurt Warner rather than just sort of *being* Kurt Warner.

Humbly recognizing our need for a redeemer is central to the Gospel. That recognition leads to things like genuine thankfulness and a self-effacing manner that may make a 30-minute enthusiastic retelling of one's life story a non-thing. It's not my place to say whether Warner's speech was wrong in some way, it just didn't "do anything" for me, as speeches go.

I guess I just wish that at some point a Christian athlete would say some version of the following: "Thanks for this honor. I had a great time playing football. Have a great night." That, to me, feels like the most "Christian" Hall of Fame speech imaginable.

Skipping PoliSci 101: A Weekend Guide to Politics-Free Professional Football

If you feel like coverage of the National Football League (and the social media surrounding it) has turned into a weird, freshman Political Science course, here are some non-political weekend pro football options:

Move the Sticks Podcast, NFL.com
What It Is: A podcast featuring two former NFL scouts—Daniel Jeremiah and Bucky Brooks—which approaches football from a scout's perspective. This is an excellent "all ball" podcast, with occasional priceless references to '90s hip-hop (Jodeci, anyone?) by a middle-aged white guy (Jeremiah).

GM Street Podcast, TheRinger.com
What It Is: Another all-football podcast featuring former NFL general manager Mike Lombardi who has deep and abiding love for the movie *Goodfellas* (note to my students: don't watch this) and isn't afraid to "go at" people in his industry (see: Pedersen, Doug). I've been involved in the game as a player or coach my entire life, but still find myself learning a lot from Lombardi each week.

2 and Out CFL Podcast, The CFL Podcast Network
What It Is: A metalhead rock radio host (Travis Currah) with a passion-for and exhaustive-knowledge-of the Canadian Football League guides listeners through the week's

matchups, and reviews the previous week. Here's what I love about this pod: Currah and his co-hosts (sometimes John Frazier, sometimes Brazilian Ty) strike a *perfect* balance between genuine love for the game, and the realization that football is absolutely *not* the end of the world. I wish more people struck this balance.

Saskatchewan vs. Toronto, CFL

Interesting People: The Saskatchewan Roughriders recently signed former Alabama star and NFL bust Trent Richardson. It's easy to snarkily make Trent Richardson jokes, but the CFL has successfully rehabbed a lot of careers and Richardson's may be the latest. Fun fact: Former Texas legend and Heisman Trophy winner Vince Young had a cup of coffee with Saskatchewan in training camp earlier this season.

Toronto Argonauts running back James Wilder Jr. is better than a good half of the backs on NFL rosters, and also better than all of the running backs on the Indianapolis Colts. He's tall, fast, and physical, with a running style reminiscent of a young Eddie George, or, in fact, a young James Wilder Sr. He'll be enrolled in PoliSci 101 (read: signed to an NFL contract) before the end of the season.

Toronto's head coach is an eccentric intellectual named Marc Trestman who is an architect of interesting passing offenses, has resurrected the career of a great CFL quarterback named Ricky Ray, and has been delightfully mum on the following topics: Donald Trump, politics.

Uniform Aesthetics: Saskatchewan's simple green-and-white uni is one of the most pleasing in a league full of simple, great-looking uniforms. Toronto is famous for its shades-of-blue aesthetic, and its dark-blue helmet is the best in pro football, in any league. Caveat: if they wear their all-white uniforms, said-uniforms look distinctly pajama-like.

Streaming: Any Given Sunday

What It Is: A mostly-mediocre professional football movie made by director Oliver Stone, who was in that "I don't edit my movies anymore" portion of his career (meaning that the movie is about an hour too long and still has an unfortunate scene featuring a player having his eyeball knocked out during a game). That said, it's bad in (ironically) many of the same ways that the NFL is bad right now: you don't care about any of the characters, it does social commentary in ham-fisted ways, and it is allegedly-interesting but actually super boring.

Interesting Player: This movie really shines in its cameos, including, but not limited to the following: rapper LL Cool J, Bill Bellamy (see: *MTV Jamz* from the '90s), Dick Butkus, Terrell Owens, Johnny Unitas, Lawrence Taylor (who was low-key brilliant as Shark Lavay, a broken-down linebacker risking his life for one more payday), and legendary running back Jim Brown who frowned and grumbled a lot which is to say that he was basically playing himself.

Uniform Aesthetics: Uniforms in this film are mostly overdone trash, making them startlingly similar to the currently unwatchable versions of the Atlanta Falcons, Seattle Seahawks, and Cincinnati Bengals uniforms. However, the Miami Sharks uni is a clean, simple beauty, and the film featured the first appearance of what would go on to be a juggernaut brand of lingerie for men: Under Armour.

Book That Most of the Film's Content is Lifted From: *You're Okay, It's Just a Bruise,* by former Oakland Raiders team physician Rob Huizenga. This is one of the best and most honest books about pro football ever written.

Awesome Aesthetic Thing: Old AstroTurf.

Redemptive Element: This may be my favorite Al Pacino performance of all time. He plays a morally-conflicted head coach whose prime years may have passed him by. Pacino's "die for that inch" locker room speech is enough to keep your remaining eyeball glued to the screen.

YouTube it, at least.

On Being the Quarterback's Father

There is a particular combination of elation and misery that comes with the office of Quarterback's Father. You'll find this man either along the top row of the bleachers, standing alone or perhaps pacing by himself along the fence because, as they say in other overly-dramatic situations, it's lonely at the top.

That said, I coached my son for several years and he never played quarterback for me. He was a battering ram of a fullback, and a heat-seeking-missile of a linebacker. But never the quarterback. Never the guy who has his hands on the football on every play. It took moving ten hours south, joining a new school, and starting football the day we moved into town for all of that to happen. And we didn't ask for any of it. There was no politicking, there were no films shared via email with the coach, and really no dialogue with the coach at all. This (not interfacing with the coach) has been pure joy, being that we just moved out of a "Daddyball" community where every father wore lots of UnderArmour gear and was heavily involved. And regarding the coach, he is right out of Southern Football Coach central casting—big, lumbering, yells a lot, runs long practices, runs three plays total, and probably has a shrine to Paul "Bear" Bryant in the narthex of his home.

But so, regarding being the quarterback's father: When your son plays a regular position like fullback or middle linebacker, you don't have the conflicting emotions of dread and excitement on every single play. There is the vague sense that he could make a great play, or make a mistake, but with a quarterback, those are multiplied tenfold. My son started his first game as the 7th grade quarterback last night, and after a few plays I was by myself, pacing along a fence. We were playing against a very tony, upscale $10,000 a year private school that may or may not have been built to avoid racial integration. The officiating crew appeared to have been alumni of said school. Their field was nicer than any grass field I ever played on at any level of football. It had a manicured hedge row around it.

Incidentally, two of my most awful experiences as a professional writer have involved famous quarterbacks and their less-famous evangelical fathers. In retrospect, God's good and sovereign hand was evident in both situations. Oddly, last night's experience gave me a strange sympathy for both men and, by the grace of God, the wounds from those experiences are long healed and mostly forgotten. But I felt sympathy, I guess, because of the visibility of their son's position and the accompanying stress. Because of the fact that whenever their sons fumble a snap or throw a ball into the dirt, everybody is looking at them.

My son did fine. He and his teammates played and fought valiantly, in spite of some very dubious officiating (two "defensive holding" calls on successive running plays? Really?) and also some dubious play-calling (see: three-play playbook). It was, all things considered, a beautiful night of football but, being that it's junior high football, the kids were required to act as though they'd just had a family member die. No smiling or laughing or talking on the bus ride home, even though they're kids who just played an amazing game and have their whole lives in front of them to be glum and quiet and surly and disappointed about a litany of things way more important than this. This is a football tradition that I hate.

On my way out I caught the eye of the 8th grade quarterback's father. His son played a brave and sensational game, but lost by two points. He spent the entire evening standing alone at the edge of the bleachers. "Which one is your son?" I asked.

"Number seven, the quarterback," he replied.

"He's a heckuva player. Played a heckuva brave game tonight," I said.

And then he looked me in the eye and said, "Thank you sir. Thank you so much. That means a lot."

And that is why I love football.

Three Sporting Events : A Retrospective
Originally Published in *The Jackson Sun*

Mayweather vs. McGregor

Watching Floyd Mayweather, Jr. fight Connor McGregor last weekend was less like watching a fight and more like paying to watch two extremely rich men who I don't know personally conduct a televised business transaction. It was as nonviolent as a world-class boxing event could possibly be, and Floyd Mayweather's halfhearted attempt at shoving his opponent after the bell in an early round suggested that the whole thing may have been a farce of billion-dollar proportions.

I felt vulnerable in that moment. Like a sucker.

That said, my house was full of friends (which is always a joyful thing) and it felt like a "cultural event" less because it was *actually* a cultural event and more because there was just a constant barrage of noise suggesting that it was one.

This will, hopefully, be the last Floyd Mayweather fight I ever order. I've done it more than once and have regretted it each time.

Rams vs. Chargers — Week 3, NFL Preseason

This is the event I should have watched all of, rather than clicking over to the Mayweather/McGregor spectacle.

On August 23, the Los Angeles Chargers signed former Lane College defensive end Whitney Richardson. I work with the long snappers at Lane, and had my first significant conversation with Whitney last season during a practice that had been driven inside by rain. He asked insightful questions about my writing and coaching life which (question asking) is an *extremely* rare thing for college students to do—especially college students who are also football players.

I also noticed that Whitney had an NFL frame in the mold of newly-minted Hall of Fame pass-rusher Jason Taylor. He went on, last season, to collect 17.5 sacks in ten games and be named the NCAA Division II Defensive Player of the Year. Whitney declared early for the NFL Draft and went undrafted and unsigned . . . but there was great excitement upon seeing his name in small print in the "Transactions" section last week. There was even more excitement when we saw him, in uniform, at the L.A. Coliseum.

Senior Day was one of the sweetest, saddest moments of the Lane season last year. In it, each senior was introduced and when their "career aspirations" were read aloud, each one indicated that they wanted to play in the NFL, which caused defensive line coach Dorsett Davis (who played in the NFL) to turn to me and ask, "When did we stop dreaming?" It was a really good question for which I didn't have an answer.

This weekend Whitney was, in a way, living all of our dreams.

The Jackson Generals vs. (I think) The Chattanooga Lookouts on a Sunday Afternoon

I am an introvert by nature and a weekend full of people-related things (the Mayweather fight party included) really taxed my reserves, people-wise. That said, a Sunday afternoon Jackson Generals game was the perfect antidote. Being that it was a late-season afternoon start on a Sunday, we had an entire upper-deck section to ourselves.

I carried on a vibrant, innings-long conversation with my wife in which the only "distraction" was occasionally checking to see if our pitcher maintained his no-hitter. I killed a spider on a railing for my wife and, in doing so, dropped my sandal into the lower deck. It was returned by a kind usher.

My oldest son got a game ball from a player and then later, a stunningly nice usher brought a ball to my younger son in what definitely qualifies as an "above-and-beyond" customer-service moment.

While many might argue that the stadium's view of I-40 may be less-than-charming, I would respectfully disagree. On a warm-but-not-humid afternoon, surrounded by the people I love, I can't image a place I'd rather be.

FanDuel, DraftKings, and
the Face of American Self-Loathing

I used to occasionally cover fights in Las Vegas and, as such, got a ringside seat (as it were, pun intended) to what real, deep-seated and chronic self-loathing looked like, being that Las Vegas was (and is) the self-loathing capital of the free world. Simply stated, Vegas is an easy place to ruin your life in a variety of ways.

So it was in the middle of like the 84th straight hour of advertising for "one-week fantasy football! Get paid immediately!" that I realized what I was seeing in ad after miserable ad: The Las Vegas male. Both companies—FanDuel and DraftKings—offer legalized sports gambling in America, which you used to have to go to a sportsbook in a Las Vegas casino to do. Now it's available to anyone with a computer, and this is why roughly an hour of every three-hour NFL telecast seems to be dedicated to ads for both companies.

The ads are the same in that they include a guy speaking who is supposed to look "regular" in that his face is a little shiny and a little bloated and a little bit like yours. He's wearing a hoodie or a t-shirt. He is 28 or 32 or 26 or 35 years old. He is the age you are. That's the point. He probably, like you, spends his professional life glued to a computer and then, according to the ad, spends his free time glued to a different computer "just picking his players and getting paid immediately." He has a slightly predatory look in his bulbous eye like if he were in Vegas for his buddy's bachelor party and if, you know, things went well he'd, you know, probably try to sleep with your cousin or your sister or your daughter and then go back to his suite and guffaw about it with his other friends who are also just picking their players and making money.

He's super clever and so are his friends.

What's disconcerting is that the youngish, dirtbag American male no longer has an obvious "look" inasmuch as he no longer has tattoos or long hair or some obvious "tell" — the likes of which your mother used to tell you to avoid. The new self-loathing American male probably went to college and has a decent job. What's interesting is that they obviously and intentionally didn't use attractive or charismatic people in these ads, rather, they cast the guy next door (subtext: your next-door neighbor is just picking his players and getting paid immediately, so why aren't you?).

Other images in the ads: Guys having fun in bars. High fiving. A giant cardboard check. Male guffawing. Money wafting down from the heavens. More male guffawing.

There's something Pavlovian and also just plain relentless about these companies and ads. They're on, literally, all the time during any sort of male-oriented television or radio programing. They're just waiting for you to relent and enter the discount code. They know that you will, eventually. They know that you'll be back next week because you want the games to quote/unquote Mean Something and you think that putting a little money on these players will render meaningless games meaningful.

What they're promising is, of course, "action." And the role that action plays is that it promises to make otherwise boring lives a little less boring. Except that in pursuing the "action" (substitute booze, drugs, cheap sex, pornography, etc. here) the pursuer always wakes up feeling a little bit less satisfied and looking a little bit more hollowed-out and Vegassy and sad in the same fashion as the guys in these ads. Somehow, you know it isn't going to go well for the guys in these ads. You intuit that they're probably mediocre at their jobs and their wives probably hate them for extremely legitimate reasons. Even though it is raining cash on their heads, in the ads, something inside reminds you that you're looking at a loser.

You may be asking, "What makes you any different, Kluck?" And my answer is absolutely nothing. I have known just enough of potentially life-ruining Vegas-style idiocy that these ads are actually terrifying to me. Looking at the guys in these ads is like looking in the mirror at an un-redeemed, un-Christ-like, bitter and hopeless version of myself. It's chilling.

There's nothing as sleepless and dissatisfied as a Las Vegas morning. The only answer to it is to take a hot shower and get on an airplane as quickly as possible, so you shuffle into the airport and find your gate, walking past other miserable looking guys exactly your age, wearing your super-unique t-shirt and your facial hair, who are miserable for exactly the same reasons—because the *action* they so desired left them feeling dissatisfied and guilty.

It's hard to end an article like this without becoming overtly evangelical and, in doing so, probably turning some people off. But really the only way to end it is by saying that with each passing day I'm reminded how much I need Jesus, and how much I want to be with my Father. We live in an era that offers absolutely everything.

There's no desire, really, that I can't fulfill with a mouse click. Except the desire to be able to live with myself. To be able to look in a mirror and not see Super Clever Vegas Man looking back.

Watch CFL Quarterback Chris Streveler

Originally Published in *The Jackson Sun*

Dear Readership: The most exciting professional quarterback you'll watch this summer and fall plays for the Winnipeg Blue Bombers in the Canadian Football League. Note that I didn't say the best. There are better quarterbacks than Streveler all over professional football, including in his own league (Mike Reilly) and other leagues (Tom Brady et al). That's not the point. The point is that you will have more fun watching Streveler than you'll have watching a litany of other quarterbacks.

Full disclosure: Do I maybe just want to be the first American columnist to heap praise on Streveler, such that when he comes south in two years and takes the NFL by storm, I can take credit for having said it first? Maybe. Do I think Streveler is good enough to do that? Absolutely.

Here's a Chris Streveler primer: split time between quarterback and wide receiver at the University of Minnesota, where he graduated with a degree in kinesiology. Transferred to South Dakota, where he rewrote school and conference records in terms of passing yards and total offense and garnered a truckload of All-America honors. Ran 40-yard dashes in the 4.4s and 4.5s. Went undrafted because he's 6'1", played at South Dakota, and, to steal a phrase from *Moneyball*, football thinking "is medieval."

Here's a short list of pro quarterbacks that Streveler will be more exciting than, this season:

- Kirk Cousins, who just exceeded the gross national product of Greece, but if history is any indicator, may helm the Vikings to a 9-7 record.

- Johnny Manziel, who circa two weeks ago was the most exciting quarterback in the CFL, despite having never taken a regular season snap in the CFL.

- Baker Mayfield, who probably won't play this year in Cleveland.

- Tyrod Taylor, who probably will play this year in Cleveland.

- Eli Manning.

- Anyone named Josh (which list includes Rosen, McCown, and, cringe, Allen).

- Anyone named Matt (Stafford or Ryan, though this one was close/tough). The thinking here is that both of these players are elite talents who have never really lived up to their potential—although Matt Ryan has gotten the closest.

- Anyone named Andy. Fun fact about Andy Dalton: Marvin Lewis is still the coach of his team, the Cincinnati Bengals.

- Anyone playing quarterback in the state of Florida: Jameis Winston (who's suspended), Ryan Tannehill (who's limited), and Blake Bortles (who is Blake Bortles).

Here's a short list of pro quarterbacks that Streveler is analogous to:

- Lamar Jackson, who will spend the requisite half-season sitting behind Joe Flacco, but who should really be starting in Week 1.

- Cam Newton, who is like a giant Streveler.

- Russell Wilson, who runs around in the pocket more and has played in more Super Bowls than Streveler.

- Rookie-year RG3, in terms of having freakish straight-line speed and a good arm.

- Deshaun Watson, whose first two games in the NFL were less impressive than Streveler's first two games in the CFL.

- Carson Wentz, who is a bigger Streveler with one more Super Bowl ring.

Here's what Streveler has done in his first three CFL starts: 570 passing yards, 6 TD's, 2 INTs, in addition to 183 rushing yards and a pair of scores. None of which tells the story, really. What makes a player exciting?

- Newness. Streveler is the first pure rookie (that is, his last game was in college, last season) to start in the CFL since CFL legend Anthony Calvillo in the early '90s.

- The ability to do multiple things at a high level— for Streveler, Lamar, and Cam Newton, this means passing and running.

- The ability to do one thing freakishly well (see: Tom Brady, passing, or Mike Vick, running).

- Exceeding expectations. When Winnipeg's starter went down, nobody expected much of Streveler. He has been a surprise.

- Being a surprise.

- Elevating an otherwise mediocre team. Time will tell, on this one.

The point here is, there's fun football and great quarterbacking to be watched *right now,* if you're so inclined. Because he is a rookie, Streveler's performances will be up and down, but early returns are good. He's also an exceedingly fun choice for the CFL's "Live Mic" games, which is yet another example of brilliant, better-than-NFL marketing by the Canadian league.

Finally, here's a short list of stories in the broader sports community that Streveler is more interesting than:

- The LeBron James free agency. LeBron is the most consistently boring dominant player in sports history. He moves the emotional needle not even a little.

If you start now, you have fifteen more opportunities to watch Streveler play this summer. Will he go on to be the next Warren Moon or Doug Flutie, meaning formerly dominant CFL quarterbacks who went on to exemplary NFL careers? It's hard to say. But wouldn't it be cool if he did?

The Day the Super Bowl Died: On Ray Lewis, *Downton Abbey*, and Growing Old

I became a grown-up tonight. I became a grown-up in part because I realized that an event that I'd once looked forward to and once placed upon a pedestal had become a boring parody of itself and also, in part, because like all grown-ups my enjoyment of the ridiculous spectacle was in direct competition with the kinds of problems that nibble around the consciousness of grown-ups.

Caveat: I love football. I probably love it too much. But I told my wife at the end of the night, "The best part about the Super Bowl this year was the cheese dip you made." I meant that. It was the only part of the evening that I enjoyed without qualification.

Tonight, of course, was Super Bowl night. A night that featured the following:

- A now-obligatory six-hour pregame show which featured the same obligatory depressing/inspiring human interest story, the same rags-to-riches story, and the same back-slapping guffawing and jocularity as last year's six-hour pregame show.

- A now-obligatory endless halftime show featuring Beyoncé wearing a leather bathing suit and wondering, rhetorically, if I'm "ready for this jelly." At which point, I turned to our friends and said the following: "I don't mean to sound smug and superior but I'm pretty sure this halftime show is evidence of the decline of civilization." I'm pretty sure I sounded smug and superior.

- Our nation's secular/spiritual Authority On Every-thing, Oprah Winfrey, voice-overing a commercial that was meant to make us reflect on something important, but which ran right after Beyoncé ex-plaining the origins of everything important she owns ("I bought it."—Beyoncé) The placement of Oprah's heavy-handed over-preachy commercial seemed strangely appropriate.

- Too much coverage of Ray Lewis, who has a strange public relationship with God and about whom way too much has been made. I cared very little about either team but was actively rooting against Ray Lewis for reasons that even I can't exactly articulate but which may have something to do with the fact that God, to Ray Lewis, seems like He may not be anything more than the guy who helped him beat a murder rap and is helping the Ravens win football games.

- The growing realization (by me) that analysis like the paragraph above probably won't ever find its way into anything I'm writing for publication these days given that it's (ed. Note: "too cynical") and (ed. Note: "smacks of negativity—please change"). There's perhaps nothing sadder and more grown-up than realizing that you're probably never going to positively change the industry you're in, and that working adulthood is a minefield full of the kinds of compromises you make just to remain em-ployed. These are the sorts of realizations that made our dads occasionally sit in a chair and just stare off into space.

- What's difficult in the above paragraph is realizing that now, I'm the dad in that vignette, and that even though I am fully thankful for the opportunity to write about athletes, I still grieve what's left on the cutting room floor at the end of it.

- My wife noticing that after scoring a touchdown, Colin Kaepernick kissed his own bicep, prompting her to ask, "Why is Kaeperdink [SIC] kissing his bicept?" She always adds a "t" to the end of "bicep" and I never correct it, because I think it's cute. Moreover, why *did* he kiss his own bicep?

- A weird power-outage in the third quarter which prompted my dad to text, "I bet Obama pulled the plug," which prompted me to respond, "Now he can raise taxes and create a government program to restore power to the Superdome." This is the kind of text exchange that only happens between old men.

What I'm hesitant to admit is that at 9 PM, while the game was still very much up in the air, I clicked over to PBS to watch Masterpiece Classics' *Downton Abbey*, a show to which I'm moderately addicted even though after last week's episode I said to my wife, "I'm never watching this again." For an hour I lost myself in the tension between Robert and Cora, wondering if Mr. Bates was finally going to get out of jail, and enjoying the fact that Mrs. Patmore was able to help the girl who used to be a prostitute cook a good meal for Matthew's mother's luncheon. I chose all of this over Super Bowl Roman-

Numeral-Whatever, which is either an indictment of the Super Bowl or proof of *Downton Abbey's* greatness. Probably both.

At the end of the evening I understood, for the first time, why my dad stopped caring about all this stuff at some point, even though he never stopped loving football. It's because he was worried about me. It's because he was probably preoccupied with his own career compromises.

It's because sometimes sitting in a chair and staring out into the void is better than whatever is on television, even if it's the Super Bowl.

VIOLET CRAWLEY
#52 – DOWAGER COUNTESS

A Decade Later,
Fantasy Football Is Still the Worst

Originally Published in *The Jackson Sun*

I hadn't played fantasy football in ten years or more, and was lured back in because I host a sports podcast called Happy Rant Sports and my co-host thought it would be fun to have a show-related fantasy football league. Spoiler: It isn't fun, because fantasy football is the worst.

For the uninitiated: fantasy football is a thing wherein you choose real players and get "points" based on their real performance. At its most innocent it's just another way to be a Passionate Fan of NFL football. Here's what it actually is for most people: another way to gamble.

I knew fantasy football was still the worst midway through tonight's Monday Night Football game in which I was listening to a "B" crew that should have been doing Tuesday *MACtion* on ESPN, and waiting to listen to an "A" crew that should be doing *Friday Night Fights* live from the Merrillville, Indiana, Casino.

I knew fantasy football was still the worst when I heard myself making comments about how terrible Matthew Stafford was at football while, in that selfsame moment, knowing full well that Matthew Stafford is actually one of the best football players on the planet and is eons better than I ever was on my best day at playing or thinking about football. This is a real thing that I feel ashamed of.

I knew fantasy football was the worst when I surveyed

the Bataan Death March that was my team this weekend: RB Jeremy Hill, out for the season with an ACL tear. RB LeGarrette Blount, probably out for the season with an ACL tear. RB Leonard Fournette, gimpy hamstring. QB Matthew Stafford, may have actually died for a few minutes during the third quarter against the New York Angels of Death, only to return to throw his fourteenth interception of the evening. Matthew Stafford is a very tough guy, regardless of his football ability.

I knew fantasy football was the worst on draft night when I got to see what it sounds like when a random 40-year-old guy in my fantasy league talks trash to my fifteen-year-old son via the online trash-talking module that comes with our league (all of these things are signs of the impending apocalypse in this writer's cynical opinion):

> **Me:** Don't say anything . . . let it go.

> **My Son:** [typing sounds, i.e., the sound of him not letting it go]

Imagine a bunch of nameless, faceless middle-aged people (and one fifteen-year-old) trying to out-clever each other on a message board. This is what utter despair looks and sounds like. All of our cleverness—all of the ones and zeroes—out into the ether. Everyone is so incredibly clever! So funny! With so much to say!

Note: My team is called "SlipperyWhenAlouette" which is super clever. My son's team is, yet more cleverly, called "TheoRiddicklySpeaking."

Fantasy football is the worst because if dehumanizing things are bad, then fantasy football is the most dehumanizing thing because it reduces actual people to the (literal) sum total of their accomplishments from week-to-week. Of all the dehumanizing things about football, this is probably the worst thing.

Remember when there was no fantasy football and no Sports Twitter and nobody really had anything super clever to say? Remember when the idea of fat, middle-aged people "drafting" world-class people and then caring passionately about their performance wasn't even a twinkle in our fat, middle-aged eyes?

I do, and it was awesome.

PART IV: GUT CHECK

Dawn of a New Era: Asian Dawn Brings Hope to Chicago's Public Schools, Creates Controversy

By: Ted Kluck for *Time Magazine*
Dateline: October 1, 1987

The air is thick with two specific smells on a sticky September morning in Chicago's Chinatown neighborhood—chicken and peas.

"Chicken and peas—that's what makes our pastries special," explains Nathan "Ping Pang" Huizenga, owner of the creatively-named "Chinese Bakery" and Executive Director of a controversial 501I(3) nonprofit organization called Asian Dawn. His hot, steaming pastries, each embossed with a coconut cross, are all the rage in the Chicagoland area. "You wouldn't think chicken and peas would be a magical combination, but it totally is," he says. "Especially with the sweet pastry. Call it Asian-Dutch fusion."

"I'm Chinese-Dutch," Huizenga explains from behind an expansive oak desk, offset, thematically, by a recently-plucked chicken hanging in his office window. Huizenga is a fit 35—he explains that he recently bought a Solo-Flex™—and sports a dazzling array of kimonos, which he wears new each day and then discards, his one affluent indulgence.

"I just like the feel of new imitation silk against my body each morning," he says, taking the plastic off a new kimono and draping it across the shoulders of a visiting writer. A tall, rawboned blonde woman named McKenna Van Vandersma, 22, arrives at 10:15 each morning with an elaborate tea service, punctuated by the former Cornerstone University volleyball player removing a chopstick from her hair bun and then letting it (the hair) sort of *cascade* down her shoulders.

"It's my favorite part of the morning," Huizenga explains, while boyishly cocking an eyebrow and playfully but also conspiratorially saying, "Eh?"

Huizinga, a youth ministry major with a minor in international finance at Cornerstone University in Grand Rapids, Michigan, never thought he would find himself at the center of an international maelstrom of controversy.

"I just wanted to help people," he says, gesturing to a box of nunchucks stacked against an office wall. "This is how it all started."

Nunchucks are a primitive weapon of Okinawan origin featuring two sticks joined in the middle by a chain or a rope. They are, in addition to being deadly, totally fun to play with.

Huizenga began importing souvenir nunchucks from Da Nang, and using them to arm students against bullies in the Chicago Public School District (CPSD). He stands and begins, impressively, swinging the nunchucks around his office and doing the thing wherein the user swings the chucks under his arms and sort of catches them on the other side. He can do it really fast.

"I gave these children some basic nunchuck training starting in kindergarten and increasing in complexity through middle-school," he says. "We nearly eradicated bullying in the Chicago Public Schools."

But Huizenga's success was not without its share of criticism. Chicago activist, poet, and performance artist Nadia Bolz-Weber has been particularly vehement in her criticism of Huizenga, even going so far as to write and stage a one-woman show entitled, "The Ping Pang Monologues," which had a two-night run at a small community theater in Chicago's Pilsen neighborhood.

The *Chicago Sun-Times* reviewed "The Ping Pang Monologues" as "uneven, at times and patently unwatchable at others." Community theatre records show that Bolz-Weber grossed $13 during the play's run.

"The answer to violence is not more [expletive] violence, even if in some cases it is totally effective and totally eradicates the original violence such that the original violence doesn't even exist anymore," Bolz-Weber explains from her office, which is actually a small space she rents in a Kinko's Copymat in Wheaton, IL.

Bolz-Weber has garnered local renown for writing one-sentence diatribes and hanging them up around the city, often several times per day. She calls this her "job." Many of those diatribes are against the Nakatomi Corporation, the one thing on which Bolz-Weber and Huizenga can agree. Chicagoans, it should be noted, mostly find Bolz-Weber shrill, crass, and aggravating, and wish she would go away.

"Nakatomi wanted to be the sole supplier of our nunchuck operation, which has spread to Indianapolis, Cleveland, Springfield, IL, and several other smaller cities," Huizenga explains. "Instead, I went with Lahaye Armaments, out of Colorado Springs—via their Da Nang office—because they could provide a weapons-grade souvenir nunchuck experience at a fraction of the price."

That decision did not sit well with Nakatomi CEO Joseph Yoshinobu Takagi, who has a longstanding and complicated relationship with Huizenga.

"I dated one of his daughters for a minute," says Huizenga. "It got weird."

Takagi embarked on a media smear campaign, using such publications as *Jet, Seventeen,* and *Inside Sports* to attack Huizenga's character, calling Huizenga an "international playboy," and even going so far as to suggest that Huizenga was shipping cartons of nunchucks to international terrorist cells including the sinister East German Volksfrei Movement.

Huizenga immediately dismisses the "international playboy" distinction, explaining that he has a "very specific type," indigenous only to West Michigan." But his silence on the Volksfrei Movement speaks volumes. On record he will only say that he is developing a "higher end nunchuck for non-scholastic use."

For Bolz-Weber, her opposition to Takagi and Nakatomi is less nuanced. "I'm against the [explective] Nakatomi Corporation because they are a corporation that makes a lot of [expletive] money and employs a lot of people, so clearly they are evil," she says. "I went to college with Nathan. He's better than that."

On his college years with Bolz-Weber, Huizenga will only say, "She was super annoying and almost nobody on campus liked her."

Huizenga's controversies aren't limited to international business and light weaponry. He has been linked to

cocaine-fueled parties in Lake Tahoe, Nevada and Grand Rapids, Michigan, and is often photographed in nightlife settings with Nakatomi Vice President Harry Ellis. To this, Huizenga only replies: "Show me a businessman in 1987 who isn't doing mountains of cocaine each morning, and often mid-afternoon just to provide a little additional 'pep.'"

At the close of business each day, Huizenga slips behind the wheel of a richly appointed Cadillac DeVille for his long commute home to a cul de sac in Winnetka—a suburb on the city's north side. The DeVille is triple-parked. "I hate how they do this in Chinatown, but what can you do?" he asks, with a shrug.

Huizenga is mum when asked why he didn't just name the bakery Asian Dawn, which would have made all kinds of sense.

On the long trip home through Chicago's diverse neighborhoods, schoolchildren can be seen walking home with a backpack slung over one shoulder, and a set of Asian Dawn nunchucks slung over the other.

"It feels good," says Huizenga. "Just knowing that I've made a difference."

Evangelical Smackdown

Wow folks, I have to say a hearty thank you from *Ted Wins* headquarters for the snark and thoughtfulness contained in your responses. The part about John Eldredge turning into a hawk was absolutely brilliant, as was the bit about the emergents turning down the lights, eating veggie wraps and emoting about the nature of conflict in general. It's all about the dialogue people. It's all about learning. Remember that.

But unfortunately, at *Ted Wins* it's all about fighting. That's why you're here. And the first rule of *Ted Wins* is "Don't Talk About *Ted Wins*." And the flood of response from Popular Evangelicals was so strong that before we can move on to semifinals, we had to create another batch of preliminary fights. So read, ponder, and weigh in with your results . . . and then all results will be tabulated and we'll move to the semis.

Note: If you're a suit from certain noted, high-powered, big-money NYC-owned Christian publishing houses and you wish to acquire the rights to this so-as-to make it into a slickly marketed book, you'll have to talk to my lawyers. I can be bought.

Note 2: Remember it's all still just a joke. Have fun with it. Enjoy it. Nobody bleeds for real because these fighters don't have feelings. They're celebrities.

White People with Dreadlocks Division
Shane Claiborne vs. Anne Lamott in a "Living Under a Bridge for Jesus" hardcore match.

Emergent Division
Tony Jones vs. Brian McLaren

Evangelical Girl-Memoir Division
Sarah Cunningham vs. Lauren Winnerin in a "Girl Meets Fist" bare-knuckled showdown.

Popular Fiction With Crummy Theology Division
William P. Young (*The Shack*) vs. Tim Lahaye and Jerry Jenkins (*Left Behind*)

The Social-Justice Division
Jim Wallis vs. Your Sense of White Guilt in a "Who Can Make You Feel More Terrible About Being White and Suburban?" match.

Prosperity-Gospel Slime Ball Division ($49.99 PPV)
Joel Osteen vs. Joyce Meyer in a "Your Best Fight Now!" match.

Books That Became Their Own Franchises Division
Rick Warren (*Purpose Driven Life*) vs. Gary Chapman (*Five Love Languages*)

Alpha-Male Division
Mark Driscoll vs. John Eldredge

Authors With the Same Names as Old MLB Ballplayers Division
Jim Palmer (*Divine Nobodies*) vs. David Wells (a bunch of good books)

People That Are Too Busy To Fight Because They're Driving a Toyota Prius, on the Phone With Barack Obama's Staffers Division

Donald Miller vs. Tony Jones (again) in a "the Real Reason Why the Red Letters are Red" barbed-wire match.

Women That Evangelical Women Love Division

Beth Moore vs. Sarah Palin

Preachers with Amazing Accents Division

Os Guiness vs. Alistair Begg

Evangelical Singers Who Look Like Girls Division

Michael Sweet (Stryper) vs. Rebecca St. James

Rob Bell Division

Today's Rob Bell vs. the basically orthodox Rob Bell of a few years ago

And now the results . . .

The Emergent Division played out as follows: After a flurry of blog posts and responses to said posts, a Revolutionary Emergent Summit was held at an undisclosed Starbucks, and then a Manifesto was written regarding all conflict, everywhere. A press release explained that "a wonderful time of dialogue and hope" resulted. All of that to say that only Tony Jones advances from this bracket.

Driscoll destroyed Eldredge in the alpha-male division, powerbombing Eldredge through a wooden table that he (Eldredge) had made from some things he found in the wilderness. Alistair Begg wins because somebody says he played rugby, and I've known a couple of rugby players in my day who were pretty tough. They also drank lots of beer (the rugby players, not Begg and Guiness).

White People with Dreads was a hard-fought, closely-contested battle, with Lamott coming out on top because her last name almost sounds like Lamotta (as in Jake, as in *Raging Bull*). Winner beat Cunningham in Girl Meets Fist (memoirs) and, as a result, they both have new books coming out that promise to be "touching, challenging, and poignant," detailing the fight. Look for them in 2009.

Lahaye and Jenkins took Willy Young to the woodshed (sorry, easy joke, and played, probably) because there were two of them and only one Willy Young. And they used lots of sweet rapture-era weaponry and stuff. My Sense of White Guilt beat Jim Wallis in a split decision. Wallis can make me feel pretty bad, but I can make myself feel a little bit worse, as it turns out (my desk is from Ikea).

Joyce Meyer wiped the floor with Joel Osteen, as expected, and negotiated 75% of the pay-per-view take, so she did pretty well financially too. Rick Warren also wasted Gary Chapman, who, as it turns out, permanently removed "Physical Touch" as a Love Language. Warren also has a goatee, and as we all know, guys with goatees are tough.

David Wells wins in the Old Ballplayers division because well, I like David Wells, and a couple of my good friends had him as a prof at GCTS. In the Prius/Obama division, Jones and Miller decided to drag-race their Priuses (Pri-i?) but both ended up driving to Starbucks where they fought over the last lemon scone with Miller advancing. Len Sweet was there too, but he didn't fight.

In a division that garnered the most attention—Women Evangelicals Women Love—Sarah Palin who was speaking at a rally, beat Beth Moore who was in the same city speaking at a conference in the same venue at the same time (get it?). Michael Sweet also advances because I love Stryper and am not afraid to admit that.

Finally, Orthodox Rob Bell confronted New Rob Bell, who ended up choking him out with one of those studded black leather belts like you get at Hot Topic. The fight was captured for posterity and will be released as Nooma 73. Here are the matchups for the next round. Vote early and vote often. The polls are open:

- Tony Jones vs. Alistair Begg

- New Rob Bell vs. Michael Sweet from Stryper

- Sarah Palin vs. Joyce Meyer (this has main-event written all over it)

- Donald Miller vs. Mark Driscoll (Battle for the Pacific Northwest)

- Anne Lamott vs. My Sense of White Guilt

- Lauren Winner vs. Lahaye and Jenkins

Mystic Pizza Revisited: Where are they Now?

Recently Zach and I watched the seminal 1988 girls' coming-of-age dramedy *Mystic Pizza*, which follows the fortunes of two sisters and another girl who work in a pizza parlor in a coastal resort town called Mystic, Connecticut. *Mystic Pizza* is a bit of a misnomer in that most of the movie takes places in locations other than the pizza parlor. However, we thought it would be interesting to catch up with the cast of characters and see what they've been up to for the last thirty years.

Charlie "Chuck, Jr." Woolery

Charlie is the WASPY teenaged douche who drove his red Porsche through Mystic, drawing the attention of Daisy Arujo, who was the hotter, "fun" Arujo sister in that she was really pretty but not all that interested in school. In the film, Charlie was the son of *Love Connection* host and game-show tycoon Chuck Woolery, who was disappointed in the fact that he had given his son all of the advantages he never had but, in doing so, had also created a son who had never worked a day in his life and didn't know how to work.

At the end of the film, Charlie Woolery took a job in an ice cream parlor to show his blue-collar girlfriend that he did, indeed, know how to work. Not surprisingly, he hated it. Soon thereafter, Charlie came to the conclusion that everyone watching the film had already come to: they have nothing in common and the sensible thing to do, rather than try to turn Charlie "blue collar," was to try to make Daisy classy, resulting in the film *Pretty Woman*.

The two were married in a really obnoxious and ostentatious ceremony in Danbury, CT, where they live with their three insufferable WASPy children, none of whom have ever worked a day in their lives. They live lives of secret, low-grade dissatisfaction with one another in that Daisy doesn't respect her husband because he's never worked or produced anything of his own, and Charlie resents Daisy because he can sense her resentment.

Daisy can often be seen on the veranda of their 16,000-square-foot mansion, drinking directly from a bottle of wine and wishing she were back in Mystic, making pizzas.

From an aesthetic standpoint, Charlie suffers from the end of the 1980s what with his popped collars and feathered hair. The '90s were a total aesthetic disconnect for Charlie, and he longed for the days when conspicuous consumption and WASPy douchery were celebrated. As a coping mechanism, Charlie began a WASPy douche support group that meets in the basement of Danbury United Methodist Church and is attended regularly by Johnny Lawrence, Chet Danbury, and Knox Overstreet.

Steamer Woolery

Steamer Woolery didn't play a large part in *Mystic Pizza*, in that he was Charlie's younger brother and appeared only in the awkward dinner scene with the Woolery family in which Chuck expressed all the dissatisfaction with Charlie. In true "brother dynamics" fashion, Steamer picked up on this and—in addition to all the WASPy sneering he did at the dinner—parlayed that sneer into a career hosting a late-'90s re-boot of *Love Connection*. He also penned a memoir entitled *Growing Up Woolery*, which chronicled his teenage years as a regional tennis champion as well as his work on "Love Connection." Steamer Woolery is, to this day, a staple of American game show television and is beloved by all.

Tim, the Architect

In his short time on an architectural freelance job in Mystic, Tim garnered quite the reputation for using his then-toddler daughter, Phoebe, to pick up young, vulnerable local women in that way that some young women go, "Aww, look how good he is with kids." However, Phoebe got older, as all toddlers do, and when Tim was unable to leverage her early-childhood cuteness into cheap sex, his world collapsed (metaphorically speaking).

His literal world also collapsed when a nearly identical pizza-and-sex-on-the-bare-boards-of-a-house-I'm-designing scenario went bad and the entire house collapsed due to an architectural oversight on his part. He died, while the impressionable young girl escaped unscathed.

Leona, Who Owned the Pizza Parlor

Leona, in addition to being a top-notch pizza chef and an attractive, older heavyset woman, also ended up being a very savvy businesswoman. She leveraged her restaurant's appearance on an unlikely televised food critic program into a chain of Mystic Pizza franchises all along the East-ern Seaboard. She was also the only woman in the movie who wasn't irresponsible sexually, and parlayed her monogamous impulse into a long and satisfying marriage with her husband, Peter, who washed all of the dishes at Mystic Pizza. They live in a 15,000 square foot mansion in Danbury, CT where she sits on her veranda with Peter and doesn't think wistfully about Mystic, ever. In an endearing quirk, Peter still washes all of their personal dishes by hand, even though they can totally afford a dishwasher.

JoJo, Who Was the Other Girl

JoJo is still really attractive, and no longer loves her husband Bill just for his body or for any specific part of his body. The years have been less kind to Bill in that he has put on a lot of weight, but his personality and spirit still shine through. Bill is a great guy. She learned the secret Portuguese pizza sauce recipe and ventured that knowledge into a lucrative position as COO in Mystic Pizza, LLC—a Subsidiary of LaHaye Armaments.

Kat, Who Was the Other Sister Going to Yale

Kat spent much of her first semester at Yale being ruined, emotionally, over what happened with Tim, the architect. As an homage to Tim she declared architecture as a major, but her heart really wasn't in it and she dropped out. She still lives in Mystic where she works as a nanny, and still wears Yale sweatshirts all the time, which most people find sad.

Evangelical Cruise Activities

Welcome to the first annual Lifeway/Crossway/Financial Peace/Chick-fil-A/Happy Rant Evangelical Cruise. I am Ted Kluck, your captain. When I'm not writing, teaching, or running the Gut Check Press empire, I'm also an armchair cruise director. Who knew?

Day One:

1-3 PM   Going Deep: Scuba and Systematic Theology with Wayne Grudem

5-6 PM   Dinner: "Daniel Diet" menu featuring berries and roughage we found on the ground near the boat

7-8 PM   Keynote: "How to Demoralize and Intimidate Your Daughter's Prospective Husbands" with Voddie Baucham

9-11 PM   "Vegas Night!" on the main deck. We'll participate by refusing to play any casino games and also by passing out tracts to the dealers we've hired for the event!

Day Two:

9-11 AM   Lecrae and John Piper rap the entire book of Romans

11AM-12   Owen Strachan raps the entire book of Leviticus and is then given a contract as the new lead singer of The Newsboys

12-1 PM   Lunch: "Paleo" diet menu featuring fish that we clubbed to death while hanging over the side of the boat earlier in the day

1-3 PM   Wild at Heart: Beginner's spearfishing with John Eldredge

3-4 PM   Wild at Heart 2: Bragging about spearfishing with John Eldredge and then giving the spears to our adolescent sons in the kinds of contrived "manhood" rituals with which Freud would have a field day

4-5 PM   Wild at Heart 3: making you feel sheepish about your sense of quote/unquote Manhood if you're not into spearfishing with John Eldredge

5-7 PM   How to be Totally Obsessed with Wealth and Money All the Time Without Looking Like You're Totally Obsessed with Wealth and Money, with Dave Ramsey

7-8 PM   Keynote: Intro to Purchasing Your First Jet, with Dave Ramsey

8-10 PM   Free time. Redeem it by "Dating Your Wife"

10-11 PM   Owen Strachan fired as lead singer of The Newsboys

Day Three:

9-10 AM   Keynote: White Guilt—Feeling Horrible About the Money You Do Have, with Jim Wallis

10-11 AM   How to Think About Owen Strachan's Rap: A Gospel Coalition Panel

More Evangelical Smackdown

It's that time again. There's a hole in your heart that can only be filled by more hard-hitting Evangelical Smackdown ™ matchups—this time in the CCM (note to normal people: Contemporary Christian Music) arena. You may (or may not) know that I'm currently working on a book on Christian music, so I'm knee-deep in learning about this stuff. Let the mayhem begin!

Rules: The only rule of CCM Smackdown is *do talk about CCM Smackdown!* And remember, we're taking into account the fighters' actual perceived fighting abilities, not their ability (or lack thereof) to rock. This is important. The champion[7] will be given an authentic CCM Smackdown trophy at this year's Dove Awards (note: not really).

Disclaimer: This is all a joke, meant only for your entertainment. I would probably like all (okay, most) of these people if we were actually to meet in person. So as Mills Lane would say: *let's get it on!*

The "Records My Mom Had in Her Collection in 1982" Division
Amy Grant vs. Sandi Patti

The "Records I Had in My Collection in 1987" Division
Petra vs. White Heart

---

[7] Ed. Note: This means the ultimate winner of the contest, not necessarily Carman, who is (in some sense) "the Champion" per the movie he made of the same name, even though his song "The Champion," which you saw turned into a skit at two hundred youth group events, portrays *Jesus* as the Champion.

The "Different Eras of DC Talk" Division
Hip Hop DC Talk vs.Guitar/Rock/Alternative DC Talk

The"Sensitive/Emo Ambiguously Christian" Division
David Bazan (formerly: Pedro the Lion) vs. Sufjan Stevens

The "People Who Might Really Kill You if You Actually Fought Them" Division
Demon Hunter vs. Carman

> Note: I know, you're not really buying the Carman thing are you? Well, just watch The *Champion* (the feature length movie, not the music video).

The "Turned Christian Later in Their Careers After Lots of Partying" Division
Alice Cooper vs. Dave Mustaine

> Note: Mustaine could have also made the "people who might actually kill you" division. He's a crazy little redhead. I wouldn't want to fight him.

The "People Evangelicals Would Really Like to Claim as Their Own" Division
Bono vs. Bob Dylan

The "Bands That Aren't Really Christian per se but We Claim Them Anyway Because the Music is Good" Division
Kings X vs. Galactic Cowboys

Note: This division also shows the fact that my musical heyday was sometime in 1996.

The "Mass Market Boy Bands Comprised Mainly of Christians" Division
Hanson vs. The Jonas Brothers

And finally, the "People Who Totally Aren't Christian but I Wish Were" Division
James Hetfield (Metallica) vs. Phil Anselmo (Pantera)

Dead Garfield Eyes: Ted and Zach
Meet at Taylor University, 1995
(A Revisionist History)

Ted Kluck, 19, is dressing for dinner in Room 242 of Wengatz Hall on the campus of Taylor University. It is October and he has just sustained his second serious football injury. He limps a little. For Ted, "dressing for dinner" means choosing the right tight t-shirt (subtext: *I lift weights*) to wear under the right sleeveless flannel, with the right pair of baggy jeans and work boots (subtext: *I can't afford real Doc Martens*).

"What time do you guys want to go to dinner?" he asks. His friend group all lolls on a sofa. There is a popular guy, a super-smart guy, and an awkward guy. Ted's friend group is not unlike that in a John Hughes movie or a 1990s sitcom. Figuring out when to go to dinner is the chief concern in all of their lives. What they don't realize is, this is the least-stressed any of them will ever be, even though they all think they are "super busy" and "super stressed."

* * *

Across campus, Zachary Bartels, 17, a high school student from Bay City, Michigan, is on campus visiting his sister Jen. Jen and Ted don't know each other because she is a couple of years older and they run in completely different circles. Jen is probably wearing a pair of baggy overalls and a horizontal striped knit shirt of some kind, because it is the '90s and she is a girl. Zach is wearing a pair of khakis, a denim shirt (open), and a Christian-themed tee that he got a Family Christian Stores, where he works part-time. He is unaware that this is perhaps the least-cool job in the history of being a high school kid. The shirt says "Messiah" but in a way where each letter is like its corresponding letter on the kind of eye chart that you would encounter at the eye doctor. The subtext of that shirt, perhaps, is that Zach himself is the Messiah—a thought which hadn't yet occurred to young Zach.

Note: The name of Zach's sister's dorm is Gerig Hall. All Ted Kluck knows about Gerig Hall is that he doesn't know anybody who lives there.

Zach, due to an intoxicating cocktail of teenage hormone and freakish levels of insecurity masquerading as freakish levels of confidence, keeps up a steady patter of sarcasm related to Taylor—which he feels intimidated by while also feeling too cool for. It's complicated. They leave Gerig Hall with a group of Jen's friends—one of whom is a theater kid, one of whom has a weird sense of humor that is about a decade before its time, and one of whom runs cross country. Her friend group is not unlike a 2017 movie about Millennials, which wasn't even a glimmer in anyone's eye in 1995.

* * *

Ted's friend group makes its way to the Hodson Dining Commons at the same time that Jen's friend group—Zach included—does the same thing. They pass on the sidewalk in the same way that Joe Fox passed Kathleen Kelly all the time in the first act of *You've Got Mail* because they both lived on the Upper West Side in New York City but didn't know each other's identities. This is noteworthy because Ted and Zach will go on to become co-owners and co-presidents of the same wildly successful publishing company which is also funny because, in 1995, Ted had never read a book that wasn't about football. In 1995 Ted was majoring in Physical Education (subtext: *I lift weights*). The idea of Ted co-owning a boutique publishing house would have, in 1995, been a laugh-out-loud proposition to anyone who knew him.

As the two groups pass, Zach whispers "meathead" under his breath. He does this to impress the girl in Jen's friend group who is about a decade ahead of her time, sense-of-humor wise. This is the kind of girl that Ted would have really enjoyed, had he ever met her. The whispering serves the twofold purpose of letting the girl know that Zach has seen Ted and seen something funny in his appearance—funny enough to try to leverage it to get a laugh out of the girl.

Ted doesn't hear Zach's whispered wisecrack which is a good thing because, at the time, Ted had a lot of his own insecurity stuff going on vis-à-vis Taylor University, and may or may not have been looking to fight at the drop of a hat. He was hanging on by a very thin thread, emotionally. Hence the Dead Garfield Eyes.

* * *

So the orientation of the Hodson Dining Commons is as follows: It really looked cool in an almost mid-century way that nobody really appreciated at the time. So on the top level there were two big staircases leading down into the area of the Commons where students got their food and then sat at tables to eat it.

At the top of each staircase sat an elderly lady who swiped meal cards. Ted always went to the same elderly lady's line. Her name was "Mickie" and Ted liked her because they were from the same hometown and also because Ted could be counted on to forget his meal card and Mickie could be counted on to let him in anyway.

As they both jockeyed for position, Zach bumped into Ted's shoulder in the way that guys who are trying to establish themselves bump into each other's shoulders. This is a thing that almost completely goes away by the time a guy hits like 25 years old, but is fairly common in the late-teen years.

"Watch where you're going [expletive]," Ted says, also under his breath, in a way that brings a snicker from the guys in his friend group but goes unnoticed by Zach which is a good thing, given both guys' insecurities.

It's important to mention that, at the time, Zach didn't see himself fronting a publishing or media empire in the future either, though he was further along, artistically, than Ted. Zach played bass guitar in a band called Couch who sang, primarily, about how hard it was to be a high school student juggling the dual responsibilities of play practice and swim practice, because plays often coincided with competitive swim season.

Ted's dinner probably consisted of several dry chicken

breasts (subtext: *I need a lot of protein because I lift weights*), a bed of rice (carbohydrates weren't yet the enemy) and a glass of water. Ted and Zach probably both retreated to their respective friend-group tables where they both engaged in lots of loud-talking and guffawing (subtext: *We have friends, and those friends think we're funny*).

* * *

The other thing about the Hodson Dining Commons is that it abuts a grassy knoll where there sits a very large and bad piece of modern art that was donated by the kind of rich benefactor that small Christian colleges have to keep happy.

About the grassy knoll: it's the kind of grassy knoll where college guys with girlfriends go to make out at night.

About the piece of modern art: it's a thick metal pole sticking out of the ground and is about 30 feet high. You don't even have to be an English major to realize how phallic "Flexing of Florida" looks. For example, Ted is a PE major and still sees the humor in Flexing of Florida. Zach sees the humor in it, too, but they don't connect over it because they don't know each other.

* * *

What's fateful about this particular evening is that Ted and Zach both end up in the Taylor University Student Union to see the same college band—Exit 59. Here's what you need to know about Exit 59: They were all the coolest kids on campus in 1995 and are all now managing hedge funds and are no longer doing music.

The thing is, if you are Ted and Zach in the 1990s you go to an Exit 59 show for the same reason: to let your insecurity manifest as smugness and superiority.

On the appearance of Exit 59: they are wearing ironic gas station work shirts because if you are a hipster in 1995 this is a thing you feel clever about doing. The word "hipster" isn't even a category in 1995, but the spirit is still the same.

Ted and Zach both hate Exit 59 because girls like Exit 59. The music is a forgettable pastiche of Blind Melon, Big Head Todd and the Monsters, Pearl Jam, and The Cranberries (Exit 59 has a girl in it). About three songs into the set, the following happens:

"I'm gonna go into the hallway,"
> Ted tells his friend group.

"I'm gonna go into the hallway,"
> Zach tells his sister.

Ted glares at several people on the way out because he thinks that intimidating everyone will be his ticket to popularity. He is wrong. Zach sneers smugly at everyone on his way out because he thinks that smugness will be his ticket to popularity. He is also wrong, but less wrong than Ted.

They meet in a hallway that, in the daytime, serves as the place where kids line up for "The Grill" which is where you go to get a hamburger if you don't want to eat in the Hodson Dining Commons. But tonight it just serves

as a place where Ted and Zach stand to get away from Exit 59, and the dilemma wherein music is playing, and a few people are "dancing" which really means just kind of swaying around. It's really stressful.

Ted and Zach are both leaning against the hallway wall in a way that is both defeated and aggressive. Ted recognizes Zach as the guy who bumped his shoulder in the Dining Commons. Because neither of their friend groups are there, it doesn't matter all that much.

A guy walks by in a sport jacket and a scarf over a T-shirt. He's got a volume of poetry under his arm. He's the kind of guy who has maps of the Paris subway system hanging in his apartment just to impress girls. Ted and Zach have never been in his apartment, yet they both have an innate sense of this. He's the editor-in-chief of the student newspaper. He's now managing a hedge fund.

"Get a look at this douche," Zach says, out loud. Ted notices and laughs. They begin to talk.

The thing about Ted is that he enjoys talking to Zach because Zach gives voice to the kinds of side projects that Ted has always wanted to be a part of but never had access to because of his limited friend group. Almost all of the side projects—in 1995—involve making fun of the kinds of people that Ted and Zach find threatening.

Ted and Zach exchange VAX addresses because they want to start an ironic band intended to mock Exit 59. It's a joke that only the two of them will get. VAX is a primitive form of email. It's a text-based network that schools are on. Zach tries to wait 72 hours to VAX Ted, but can't wait. But the thing is, due to Ted's terrible handwriting, Zach gets the address wrong and the two don't connect.

Twelve Years Later

Ted is a writer of some renown. In an ironic twist, he now wears his own scarves over t-shirts occasionally. By "some renown" I mean that he has written three sports titles with very niche (read: small) audiences, in addition to a book about the church with Reformed superstar Kevin De-Young. The DeYoung book leads to an in-store signing event in Lansing, Michigan, that will be attended by Zach Bartels and his wife, Erin. They sit on the front row and during the "Q&A" time they ask the only questions.

Afterward, they ask Ted to lunch. The rest is publishing history.

Titles of Popular Christian Books
If You Replace One of the Key Words
with the Word "Parkour"

You know what's funny (rhetorically, speaking)? Parkour. The idea (some idiot jumping around on buildings downtown and calling it sports/art) is funny and even the word is kind of fun/funny to say. *Parkour*. Say it. This occurred to me when I was in a friend's basement theatre and that friend was playing Xbox Parkour on a larger than life-size screen, and I've been sort of thinking about it ever since. Specifically, what would happen if you replaced certain words in certain book titles with the word "Parkour." For example:

- *Mere Parkour*
- *The Parkour Driven Life*
- *Your Best Parkour Now*
- *The Case for Parkour*
- *A Parkourist's Progress*
- *Why We're Not Parkourists: By Two Guys Who Should Be*
- *Just Do Parkour*
- *Erasing Parkour*
- *Crazy Parkour*
- *Knowing Parkour*
- *I Kissed Parkour Goodbye*
- *The Parkour-Centered Life*

How Seminal '80s Movie *Dead Poets Society* Would Have Changed had it Been Written from the Perspective of Other Key Characters

As you probably know, *Dead Poets Society* is not only Peter Weir's worst movie, it is the quintessential faux-deep '90s exploration of things like passion and creativity and non-conformity and New England boys' schools. The story is told with unconventional poetry professor John Keating as the protagonist, but I wondered how the movie would change if written from the perspective of other key characters.

Chet Danbury

Public School Quarterback Chet Danbury was dating the girl (Gloria) that the Knox Overstreet character inexplicably stole from him. I say "inexplicably" because Chet Danbury, as far as we know, was a handsome, successful public-school student athlete (football), and an attentive boyfriend, given the fact that he gave Overstreet a beating when Overstreet was creepily touching his passed-out girlfriend. Also, here's all we know about Overstreet: he creepily touched her while she was drunk, and then he showed up at her school and embarrassed her—motivated, no doubt, by the questionable "teaching" of Keating. He also stole a sandwich from the cafeteria as he was jauntily exiting the school. Not cool. Also, Danbury was every bit as WASPy and wealthy as Overstreet, given the opulence of his home. Here's something you can take to the bank: You're not failing in life if your name is "Chet Danbury."

A *DPS* reboot with Chet at the center is a lighthearted romp through public high school in the 1950s, featuring Chet in some half-hearted classroom scenes, succeeding on the football field, still giving Knox Overstreet a beating, marrying Gloria, and then becoming a successful (choose one: doctor, lawyer, investment banker).

Mr. Nolan, Administrator

If you pay any attention to *DPS* at all, it's hard not to agree with the following: John Keating is a really bad teacher. Here's what we know about Keating: he played a lot of poetry kickball, he shamed introvert Todd Anderson in the classroom a whole bunch, he manhandled a bunch of other students, and he totally disrupted class when he had to return to the room to grab his "personal effects." Yeah, right. He totally knew they'd be having class then.

I'd love to make a movie celebrating the hardworking and underappreciated administrators who really make tony, upscale New England boys' schools go: The Mr. Nolans of the world.

Did Mr. Nolan have his problems? Sure. He probably didn't need to bend his students over a desk and spank them. That seems a bit extreme. But he was otherwise a devoted lifelong administrator of a very successful private school who momentarily had his life ruined by a rogue teacher. By dealing decisively with the Keating problem and mitigating against the PR issues that inevitably followed, Nolan is the real hero here.

Gerald Pitts—The Tall Guy with the Flat Top

I really liked this character. As he told the girls in the cave, "I'm either going to Yale . . . or I'm not." The burning question, for me, is: does Pitts actually end up at Yale? Does he ever find love? Maybe with one of the girls in the cave? The movie would have really flown had it focused on Pitts and not on the snively, over-dramatic Neil Perry or the mopey introvert Todd Anderson.

A word on names: I'm of the opinion that a person's name does a great deal to determine the outcome of their life. The chief problem facing Todd Anderson and Neil Perry is that they didn't have WASPily-awesome names like Knox Overstreet or Chet Danbury.

The Desk Set That Was Flung Into the River

The real heroes in *DPS* were the handsome, leather-bound desk sets and blotters that appeared all over this film. Men really knew how to set up a desk in New England in the 1950s. My reboot would be a celebration of these desk sets. Where are they produced? Why are they shrink-wrapped? Was that (shrink wrap) even a thing in the 1950s?

We went off the rails as a culture the moment the rebellious, ungrateful Neil Perry flung Anderson's desk set into the river. It was a moment in time that signaled a paradigm shift away from handsome oak desks, appointed with love and intentionality, and a shift toward the sorts of mediocre Formica monstrosities inhabited by cubicle-dwellers around the world, reclaimed barn doors (hipsters), and our current sign of the apocalypse: standing desks. Neil Perry ruined desks, and I hate him for it.

Gloria

Why would she follow a strange guy into a cave?

Neil Perry's Father, Mr. Perry

I see an action-oriented revenge picture entitled *Dead Poets Society Two: Dead Poet,* in which Mr. Perry hunts John Keating through the picturesque New England countryside, bent on avenging his son's death (which was probably Keating's fault).

Dr. Hager

Dr. Hager was the awesome colleague who often stared down at Keating from a (literal) tower of ivory. Hager was the one who waved knowingly when Keating left campus—it (the wave) was full of both smugness (good) and compassion (also good). Here's the thing: Dr. Hager is a good educator. I want a movie exploring his pedagogy and classroom management. It may not be as flashy as *DPS*, but I bet we'd all learn something.

EDITH'S HAPPY DAY

An Original Screenplay
by
Ted Kluck

INT. DOWNTON ABBEY DINING ROOM –
EVENING

EDITH CRAWLEY, LORD GRANTHAM, CORA
CRAWLEY, TOM BRANSON, MISS BUNTING,
LADY MARY CRAWLEY and the DOWAGER
COUNTESS are all seated in the dining room for a
lavish dinner.

> TOM BRANSON
> I just don't know what to think of all of
> you. I mean, don't get me wrong, I love
> eating world-class food, smoking world-class
> cigars, drinking world-class brandy, and
> never having to do anything each day . . .
> but . . . I just feel so conflicted about it.

> MISS BUNTING
> You hate them, don't you? Meaning, I hate
> them.

TOM BRANSON

I'm just undecided about it, and I think I probably will be forever, because if I'm not conflicted about this, there's kind of nothing interesting about me.

LORD GRANTHAM

Somebody do something about that hateful woman!

Edith springs from behind her placesetting and punches Miss Bunting three times in quick succession, bloodying her nose. Lord Grantham stands up and cheers.

EDITH CRAWLEY

I'm gonna punch you . . . now!

Edith punches her in the nose right when she says "now," much to the delight of everyone in the room.

MARY CRAWLEY

Edith you're the best! Everything you do is amazing! I love how you punched that shrill little harpie in the face!

CORA CRAWLEY

Sweet Edith . . . I've never been more proud of you in my entire life.

INT. DOWNTON ABBEY BASEMENT-EVENING

MRS. PATMORE has just finished giving the staff a French lesson, and is now hard at work sewing brand new custom ball gowns for all of the downstairs staff. THOMAS BARROW is in a corner chatting amicably with MR. BATES – they appear to be flipping through a scrapbook together.

                    MRS. HUGHES
        Why Mrs. Patmore, I didn't know you spoke
        French and were a world class fashion
        designer? Who taught you all of that?

                    MRS. PATMORE
        Edith did. She's the best.

Mr. Barrow pipes up from the corner.

                    THOMAS BARROW
        I used to be a hateful, vindictive jerk until
        Edith began counseling Mr. Bates and me in
        the evening. I no longer try to sabotage
        everyone's relationships, and Mr. Bates hasn't
        killed anyone in a long time.

He turns to Bates.

                    MR. BATES
        Yeah, Edith. What can I say?

The best part about all of this is that Edith is standing quietly at the foot of the stairs within earshot of all of these nice comments.

EXT. DOWNTON ABBEY – NIGHT

Edith, Mary, and LADY ROSE are all dressed in their finest gowns (made by Mrs. Patmore) and are waiting for a driver to take them into London for an evening soiree. The staff waits with them so that they don't have to wait alone.

> MARY CRAWLEY
>
> I sure am looking forward to this high-end society function in London at which there will be lots of eligible men in tuxedos.

> LADY ROSE
>
> Me too. (a beat) except for one problem.

> MARY CRAWLEY
>
> What's that?

> LADY ROSE
>
> The fact that I look fat and inadequate compared to Edith. She's the prettiest.

> MARY CRAWLEY
>
> She really is. I feel really frumpy compared to Edith too. Let's not even go.

EDITH CRAWLEY
(beaming)
No, you guys should totally go.

INT. HIGH END LONDON SOIREE - NIGHT

The Crawley women are all standing around looking
bored and attractive at the party, which features an
assortment of men approaching Edith.

TOM BRANSON
Edith, I've been doing some thinking and
while I enjoyed being quasi-homeless and
doing anarchic things, I think I far prefer
living the life of the wealthy, leisurely
aristocrat. Also, you look really hot in that
gown. Will you marry me?

Edith blushes.

THOMAS BARROW
You're so beautiful that I'm not gay
anymore. Will you marry me?

Edith blushes.

SHRIMPIE FLINTSHIRE
We might be tangentially related, but will
you marry me?

Edith blushes.

JACK ROSS

I'm about to play another set of super seductive jazz music, being that I am a super
seductive (and black) jazz musician who, if
we got together, would really upset your
parents, given my occupation and, I'll just
say it, my race. But all of that said . . . will
you marry me?

Edith blushes.

DR. CLARKSON

I know I'm your doctor, and that makes
what I'm about to say a little weird, but . . .
will you marry me?

Edith blushes.

TONY GILLINGHAM

I'm not into Mary anymore. Will you marry
me?

Edith blushes.

INT. LORD GRANTHAM'S STUDY - NIGHT

Edith enters to find her father cradling his beloved
dog, ISIS, who is dying of cancer.

EDITH CRAWLEY

What's wrong?

LORD GRANTHAM

Isis is dying. But even though I'm showing a
lot of emotion about this it is in no way
more significant to me than the fact that you
recently found out that Michael Gregson
died. I'm sadder about that. Also, I love you
more than this dog.

EDITH CRAWLEY

Oh daddy, I feel so valued when you say
that.

CARSON, the head butler, enters, carrying an ornate
card on a silver platter. He presents the platter to
Edith.

CARSON

A letter for Lady Edith.

He opens it for her while she watches. Edith waits
expectantly as Carson reads the letter to her.

CARSON
(continued)

"Dear Edith, This is Michael Gregson. I'm
not dead. Long story. Can't wait to see you
and run the publishing company together.
And also raise our child. Hugs and Kisses,
Michael"

Edith collapses into tears of joy.

EDITH CRAWLEY

This is the happiest day of my life!

CARSON

Lady Edith, that reminds me. I've given it some thought, and I no longer want to buy a cottage with Mrs. Hughes. I'd rather buy one with you. You don't have to give me an answer now.

Edith is still crying. Happily.

FADE OUT.

Interview with Duke Morrison, Head Coach, Denver Values Football Club

By: Ted Kluck for *Cigar Aficionado Magazine*
Dateline: June 5, 2019

Duke Morrison lives large. And by that I mean he is, literally, quite large—just over his listed playing weight of 262 pounds. He unfolds his substantial girth from the Ford F-12,000 Super Extended Cab he is driving, gratis, thanks to an endorsement deal with Franz Forman Ford in Golden, Colorado. Duke Morrison is a man who lives for making deals.

"Who did you say you were with, again?" Morrison asks as he brushes by me, the fabric of his officially licensed Denver Values sweats making contact with my notebook and dictophone in the Values team facility.

"These are the dress sweats," he explains, which I know is an example of the gruff humor of Duke Morrison because of the way he chuckles afterward. This is a dead giveaway that he is making a joke.

He doesn't so much clip the end of his Partagas Flor de Tabaco as hack at it, because Duke Morrison doesn't do anything small. Each finger is the size of the large bratwurst they serve on the mezzanine level at Dynex/Lifeway/Excellence-in-Christian-Publishing Stadium—the stadium that Morrison has called his workplace for the last 22 years, in that for the last 22 years he has either played or coached for the Denver Values.

Also: his Ford F-12,000 has a record-setting 11 doors.

"I enjoy life," says Morrison, who also has endorsement deals with DeWars Scotch and, with quarterback Tim Strongbow, is co-owner of a chain of In-n-Out Burgers. He pours himself a few fingers of DeWars in a Values stadium giveaway glass—the plastic kind with a picture of a player on it. In this case, the player is Ted Strongbow, which is all kinds of ironic.

"I started smoking cigars when I was a player," Morrison explains. "I would light one up in the training room after each game, when I was getting a Lydocaine injection into a broken foot that I played through for seven years. It (the cigar) gave me something to think about besides a needle going into my foot."

Morrison—ever the workaholic—didn't become the two-time Barbasol Player of the Year by standing still. He is in perpetual motion—even if today that motion includes pressing rewind on a remote control as he watches film of the Values' last game. Speaking of remote controls . . .

"Yeah it was weird when that guy put that microchip into the neck of my third string quarterback, which resulted in the best football that quarterback ever played in his life," he explains, as though he is explaining a minor bit of traffic he encountered on the way to the stadium in his F-12,000 SuperCab. This is to say that he is nonchalant about it. "But, that's football, I guess. I tell you . . . there are times I wish he still had a microchip in his neck and there was still a weird little man controlling him with a late-model Sega controller. Those were good days."

Morrison is deeply nostalgic. So much so that he married the girl who played a small role in that fateful night at Dynex-Lifeway Stadium. "I married us right here in this palatial office," he explains, before ordering two bacon cheeseburgers via his secretary. "Those were some good times—other than a kid getting halfway blown up by a grenade that detonated out in the concourse. There's a plaque out there now, adjacent to the Stadium Club Bistro and Dippin' Dots."

Cigars, for Morrison, provide a means for slowing down, and the window into the insights he shares as the world's foremost scholar on another scholar named Marcel Proust. When asked where he first acquired his passion for Proust's philosophies, he explains:

"College."

Morrison was a standout linebacker at Florida Christian Polytechnic University where he twice made All-Conference, but made the Dean's List all four years. When I ask him to elaborate on his academic success, he replies: "I did the reading. It's not that hard." And then, "Are we almost done?"

Morrison is a complex man. He maintains a tobacco plantation in Ocala, Florida, which is curated by his grown son, Troy Aikman Morrison, who was born last year. Cigars are a part of the daily rhythm of life in the Morrison household.

"My wife, Kate, smokes them too," he explains.

Indeed, she does.

Rewriting Several Key Scenes in *Karate Kid III* with Mr. Miyagi's Grammar and Other Significant Errors Corrected

TERRY SILVER

I owe you, man.

JOHN KREESE

You don't owe me anything.

TERRY SILVER

Oh, bu~~llshit~~ I don't owe you anything? What about Vietnam, huh? How many times did you save my ass?

JOHN KREESE

I don't know. I lost count. Also, given your age now, in the late 1980s, you would have been a toddler during the Vietnam War. So there's that.

* * *

MR. MIYAGI

If karate is used to defend one's honor and defend life, then karate means something. If karate is used to defend a plastic and metal trophy, karate doesn't mean anything.

* * *

INTERIOR, SINK AND VICINITY—DAY

The occupants of Terry Silver's BATHROOM have
just met MIKE BARNES.

TERRY SILVER
So what do you think?

MARGARET
Oh, he's obnoxious.

TERRY SILVER
(laughing)
Yeah. He's perfect.

Silver relaxes into bubble bath in what looks like a
giant, standard bathroom sink, which begs the obvious
question as to whether Mr. Silver has a gigantic
bathroom, to scale, or just sort of shrinks himself to
bathe in his regular, standard-sized bathroom sink.
Also, Karate Kid III is the worst movie ever made.

* * *

DANIEL LARUSSO
(tentatively)
Mr. Miyagi?

Daniel holds up the injured Bonsai tree. Thunder
crashes outside. Upon seeing this, Miyagi drops
his broom in sad shock before calmly taking the
tree and tending to it.

DANIEL LARUSSO
(worried sad)
Will it be okay?

MR. MIYAGI
It depends if the root is strong. See, what
you have here is a situation in which the
structural integrity of the Bonsai has been
damaged but perhaps there are enough
healthy roots remaining to deliver important,
life-giving nutrients to the rest of the tree. Is
that pretty much what you were wondering?

DANIEL LARUSSO
Yeah.

* * *

DANIEL LARUSSO
I know you don't believe in fighting, but
tournament karate isn't exactly fighting.

MR. MIYAGI
It's not exactly ping-pong either, which is me
making a funny quip in order to release some
of the obvious tension here. But what's ironic
in your statement is that it really isn't exactly
fighting in the sense that what will probably
happen is that Mike "Bad Boy" Barnes will
hit you all over your legs, torso, back, and
face, but then, inexplicably, the "score . . . "

(makes air quotes)

MR. MIYAGI
(continued)
. . . will be "tied"

(more air quotes)

MR. MIYAGI
(continued)
. . . and then you'll land one feeble punch to
his ribs and will then be declared the
winner.

DANIEL LARUSSO
That sounds good.

MR. MIYAGI
Hai.

Study Bibles I'd Like to See, Given Thomas Nelson's Recent Release of *The Duck Dynasty Study Bible*

The Andre the Giant Study Bible

The Zangief from Street Fighter Study Bible

The Tootie from Facts of Life *Study Bible*

The Other Girl from Facts of Life, *The One Who Is a Christian Speaker Study Bible*

The Kreese from Karate Kid *Study Bible*

The Dwight Schrute Study Bible

The "The Situation" Study Bible

The Chaz Marriot Study Bible

The "Platform" Study Bible

The Pete Rose Should Be in the Hall of Fame Study Bible

The Lloyd Dobler Study Bible

The U2 Lyrics Study Bible

The Mike Seaver Study Bible

*The Super Bowl Shuffle Study Bible feat.
William "The Refrigerator" Perry*

*The Twitter Every Word Is Hashtagged
and Every Name is Squigglied Study Bible*

*The 1986 Mets Featuring Daryl Strawberry and
Keith Hernandez and Mookie Wilson Study Bible*

The Joyce Meyer Study Bible

I Want to Go in the Hallway
(or Do You Guys See What You're Doing to the Blinds?)—Winter Blast 2010

"I feel weird. I need to go to the hallway."
—Me, at World Vision's Winter Blast™

We all have guilty pleasures. When I saw that Building 429—a Christian band that I'd heard the name of but knew nothing more about—was coming to Lansing, I booked my ticket and queried my Sherpa, Zach, about the band. He thought for a minute and replied: "Frosted tips."

"You know that band, the Goo-Goo Dolls?" he asked. I did know the Goo Goo Dolls. In fact, I really like them, guiltily. I don't have any of their albums but whenever I hear a song I always know the words to it, and I usually sing. It's not music you admit to liking in the company of guys, being that it's sung by a really attractive guy in frosted tips and an emo shirt. Goo Goo Dolls music is love songs, for dudes.

"Building 429 is sort of the Christian Goo Goo Dolls, in a frosted-tips slickness sort of way," he says.

"Do you want to go?" I ask.

"Absolutely."

The Building 429 show was actually a part of a mini-festival, sponsored in part by 88.1 Smile FM[8], called Winter

---

[8] Slogan: If you're living like there is no God, you'd better be right!

Blast (which sounds to me like a chewing gum brand . . .
ex: Try Dentyne's WINTER BLAST! Also, not to be confused with Winter Jam, which is another Christian music
festival), but is actually a multi-act show-slash-shill for
World Vision. I went to Winter Blast largely because it was
only ten dollars, I had heard of one of the bands (Building
429) and it was at a local megachurch near my house (Mt.
Hope Church) that I was really curious to see the inside of
(which ended up looking, surprisingly, a lot like a church).

Bits of Dialogue, Exchanged with Zach, Before the
Show Started:

- Upon seeing a banner with pictures of the Mt. Hope
  pastors, Zach pointed to one and said "Have you
  read his book called *Ten Ways to Survive if You Miss
  the Rapture*?" I hadn't. He went on to explain that
  one of the ten ways to survive involved stocking up
  on a lot of batteries and listening to the radio, which
  both sound like really good ideas to me.

- Me, upon entering the venue and scanning the
  crowd, the majority of whom were under 18: "I feel
  like we're chaperones at a youth group lock-in."

It would get way, way weirder. The show started with
a band called Echoing Angels, who actually ended up
being the most talented group on the entire bill. To picture
Echoing Angels, imagine the five coolest kids in your high
school youth group. Now imagine them a few years older,
with guitars in their hands. From where we sat, the front
man looked a lot like a puffier Luke Wilson—come to
think of it, a lot like Luke Wilson looks in the cell phone
ads he's doing now.

Me: "I wonder what Christian college these guys led worship at before they started doing this?"

Zach: "I wonder what mid-sized megachurch these guys are the house band for, currently?"

Echoing Angels, like I said, was the highlight of the night. They were actually quite talented and played a tight set that was too short. After Echoing Angels, Zach and I took a spin through the concourse/narthex past the merch tables, where we realized that kind of urbany/willowy font that Relevant Magazine made cool six years ago had been utilized on absolutely every piece of merchandise (shirts, CDs, hats, wristbands, keychains, glossy band photos, etc.) available for purchase.

One Immutable Law of the Universe: Lead guitar players are always tall/willowy/attractive, while bass players are always squatty, with a low center of gravity—like the kid who played offensive guard on your high school's football team. Sometimes even a little pudgy, they're the only guys not wearing skinny jeans and the only guys who look like they eat regular meals. Why is this?

We both felt very creepy/old when we both walked by Britt Nicole's merch table and both noticed a very unintentionally(?) seductively glossy photo of her in a sun dress on a bike. We both thought of Debbie Gibson, on whom we both had crushes as middle schoolers. We both felt weird. Herein lies the dilemma with young, Christian pop divas vis-à-vis unintentionally(?) selling their sexuality.

Amy Grant elicited her share of controversy over this issue early in her career, in which it seemed that she was either being praised or castigated for being attractive/interesting to look at. Her comments in a June 1985 *Rolling Stone* interview added fuel to the fire, when she said things like "I feel that a Christian young woman in the eighties is very sexual," and "I'm trying to look sexy to sell a record. But what is sexy? To me it's never been taking my shirt off or sticking my tongue out."[9]

Not surprisingly, everybody flipped out—more over a Christian *talking* about taking her shirt off or sticking her tongue out than actually doing it. Modesty has always been a tough thing to quantify. There are those who think that a Christian woman wearing anything besides a burlap jumper with an apple sewn on the front is immodest. But there are those who are clearly a little too comfortable with the world's standards in this area.

It's no secret that being attractive is part of being a rock star, Christian or otherwise. It makes me wonder what's so different between Amy Grant (or Britt Nicole) picking out the perfect "look good" outfit before a show, and Toby Mac spending eight hours on his hair and/or picking out just the right hat to wear? It's all vanity, right?

Between sets a guy who looked like Carson Daly (note: everybody in the room looked like Carson Daly, if looking like Carson Daly means wearing skinny jeans, some kind of leather jacket, and some kind of overly-contrived dishevelled hairdo) came up on stage and let us know that for $30, we would receive a Building 429 poster, a CD, a T-shirt, and "the opportunity to come backstage and pray with the band." I seriously considered doing this, for research purposes, but then cooler heads prevailed. I'm so glad I didn't (more on that later).

After offering the opportunity to pay-to-pray, Carson[10] tried to give away some free Building 429 CDs to audience members. He tried to engage them by asking if anyone knew the name of Building 429's new hit single. A couple of kids raised their hands but failed to come up with the name. At which point, he sarcastically mumbled, "Well, you guys are really devoted," and left the stage. Seriously, this happened. At which point I turned to Zach and said "That was worth the ten dollars."

Next was a set by a band called Mike's Chair. Here's what I remember about Mike's Chair: Two of the four members of the band wore yellow scarves over their sweaters. That was enough to make me want to leave the room before they even started playing. These guys looked like the kind of kids I wanted to beat up in college when I was an angry freshman at Taylor University (disclaimer: I'm sure they're great guys and good musicians). One and a half songs into their set I asked Zach if he wanted to go back out into the hallway. He did. In the hallway we found a larger-than-life-sized banner of Mike's Chair in all of their affluent/suburban/sexy/Christian glory.

Zach: "Mike's Chair looks like the kind of band that scheduled a photo shoot on the first day they formed as a band."

Me: "Mike's Chair = Dad's Money."

---

[10] Background: If you're under the age of 30 you may not know who Carson Daly is/was . . . he was a veejay on MTV back in the late '90s/early 2000s. For a while, MTV tried to create the veneer of its male veejays being "journalists" of sorts (like Kurt Loder). Carson Daly was sort of the departure from this line of thinking.

The highlight of the Mike's Chair set, according to Zach, was that they played a DC Talk[11] song from the mid 1990s, which we could hear from the plush leather divans we were sitting in, in the Mt. Hope narthex. In those divans, we had a long conversation about the type of hairdo rocked by Mike, the Mike's Chair frontman (also rocked by many of the other guys onstage throughout the night). It's a sort of moppy, blonde look not unlike, we decided, the kid on the Dutch Boy paint can, or He-Man from the He-Man cartoons in the 1980s.

We figured we would have a few minutes between Mike's Chair and Britt Nicole, but she started playing almost immediately so we went back in. She was wearing an '80s throwback outfit featuring a black T-shirt, a sort of Madonna material-girl esque puffy black skirt, and leggings. She jumped around onstage a lot and appeared to have a lot of energy. At one point she asked the members of the audience to put their hands in the air, which I did, because for a minute I felt like it was Debbie Gibson asking me to do it. (Note: Being reformed, I've never put my hands in the air for any reason, up to this point).

Britt Nicole was actually much more interesting between songs. After her first song she told the story of how she got "discovered"" by Building 429 and ended up on tour with them.

"I was standing in line at a concert to get my CD signed, just like you guys do," she said (implication: I used to be regular, just like you!). "I gave them my demo and

---

[11] I can't figure out if Zach likes DC Talk ironically, or un-ironically, because even though they went through some famously cheesy phases, he insists that they still had some good music and will defend them in an argument.

figured they'd never listened to it . . . but they *did* and now I'm on stage with them! That's what God wants to do for you!"

Cue: squeals from the audience.

Other things said by Britt Nicole: "Let me see your spirit fingers!" Zach and I, in the spirit of participation, showed her our spirit fingers (see also: things I never thought I'd do).

That (the fact that God can/wants to make all of your dreams come true) was a common theme throughout the night. A sort of prosperity-follow-your-dreams message. This would seem to be a message that would play well to the Mt. Hope audience, if the books displayed in their church bookstore are any indication.

One thing I like about Britt Nicole is the unashamed way she talks about wanting to become a rock star[12]. In an interview that ran as a part of the Creation Festival in 2008, she spoke of moving to Nashville[13] to pursue a music career. She spoke of meeting with three record labels and being rejected by all three, who all said that she "wasn't ready." She then spoke of showcasing for the same three labels a few years later, all of whom ended up offering her a record deal. "It was a blessing," she told the interviewer. "It wasn't through the labels, it was through Him."

---

[12] If the '90s/grunge/emo movement did anything, it was to create this sort of situation where you had to pretend like you didn't want the stardom to happen. We're not like this about other careers. Christian engineers don't say to themselves, "I never wanted to be a successful engineer. In fact, success is dumb." Yet we expect our rock stars to feel this way, for some reason. I appreciated Britt Nicole's "I moved to Nashville because that's where you go to get famous" brand of candor.

[13] Our (Christians') Hollywood.

It strikes me that this message, from Britt Nicole, is not unlike the success narratives that are spun by Christian athletes. In a way they give glory to God, but in a way they still paint success and fame as the "salvation experience."

She adds, "What we have with Christ is a relationship, not a religion." Groan. More bumper sticker theology.

We make it three songs into Britt Nicole's set before once again retiring to the divans in the hall, where we realized it had been 20 years since Nirvana's "Smells Like Teen Spirit" was released. Nothing like a nubile Christian girl in a Debbie Gibson outfit to make you realize how old you are.

It occurred to us that for a rock show to really be a rock show, there had to be some element of danger involved. Even if it isn't real danger, there has to be something about the music, or the environment, that puts the viewer on edge a little bit. I felt this way at the Metallica show, the Rolling Stones show, even Stryper to a certain degree. The idea that getting hit with a beer bottle or seeing some crazy fan lift her shirt was a very distinct possibility. Zach then told the story of getting mugged at a Michael W. Smith/Amy Grant concert at the Palace of Auburn Hills when he was ten years old. "A fat guy pushed me up behind a stairwell and asked me if I had any money," he recalled. "I said yes and he took all of it—like nine bucks. I cried all the way home." That, friends, is danger.

The weirdest part of the night would happen after the Britt Nicole set and before Building 429.

Jason Roy, the front guy for Building 429, took the stage immediately after Britt Nicole. Zach insisted we go in, to "catch the orientation." But growing up evangelical taught me one thing: If there's a tinkling piano in the background, there's going to be some sort of heartstring-pulling talk, followed immediately by an appeal for money and/or an appeal to come up front and get saved. Roy began by telling the audience about a trip he took to "Central America." Behind him, on a giant screen, flashed giant photos of impoverished children—the kind you always see photographed standing around emergent guys on emergent guys' blogs.[14]

We figured the talk would be short and, of course, have no problem with World Vision raising money at a World Vision sponsored event (note: I like World Vision and think they do good work; that doesn't make what follows any less weird-feeling, but I want to acknowledge that it may be my problem). They have to make the money back somehow. But the talk went on. And on.

Roy spoke about driving past shanties, which apparently reminded him of those storage-unit rental places, prompting him to ask the cabbie, "What do they store in there?" To which the cabbie replied, "People live in there, Jason." And then, finally, came the appeal to sponsor children, except that Roy sort of made it clear that the band wouldn't start playing until the packets for the ten children he was holding in his hand were sponsored. People were told to raise their hands to accept a child.

"Your gift will help these kids go to schools with

---

[14] World Vision really ought to be selling the right to photoshop yourself into these photos, which would save a lot of people a lot of money on travel, etc. It's important nowadays to be the kind of Christian who gets photographed with children like these. If you're not the kind of person who feels called to be photographed with children like these, I would question your salvation.

computers, so that they can move to the city and have a better life," he said. This was a recurring theme throughout: computers, and the city, equalling a better life. Piano keys still tinkling in the background. The poor pianist had to play for about 45 minutes straight.

It occurred to me that after spending most of my adult life in thinky. Reformed-ish churches, it had been a long time (college?) since I had experienced one of these superemotional appeals. We also realized that to be a Christian rock star/band today means linking up with one of these fundraising/help the children/social justice organizations. To be a Christian rock band without a social conscience is to be the worst kind of heel. Though I feel like a heel for writing what I've written (and am about to write).

Me: "I feel weird. Let's go to the hallway."

Zach: "No way. This is like sitting through the time share talk, so that you can stay in the condo for free. Besides, we can't go now because ushers are standing in front of the doorway."[15]

Me: "I've spent tens of thousands of dollars adopting children in Ukraine . . . why do I feel like a jerk for not spending $35 on one of these children?"

Zach: "That means it [the appeal] is working. Also, your kids are white, so . . . "

Me: "I feel like sponsoring the last five children just so we can hear the band."

---

[15] Note: Ushers were standing in front of the doorways.

Finally, it was over and there was yet another fifteen-minute break before the Building 429 set. Back out in the narthex/concourse we saw Britt Nicole[16] signing autographs for lots of 9-15 year old girls. Near her table was a group of giddy, emo-looking college guys deep into the process of not having the courage to ask for Britt Nicole's number. The Mike's Chair guys were standing in front of the giant photo of themselves. We were losing steam, rapidly, for Winter Blast. I'd never wanted to leave a place more in my life, yet I couldn't really identify why. We decided to lean against the back wall of the auditorium, where we could see the stage but be close to one of the doors to make an early exit, if necessary (hint: necessary).

We were approached by a matronly woman in an oversized T-shirt with the word USHER emblazoned on it.

"Do you guys see what you're doing to the blinds?" she asked. I didn't see what we were doing to the blinds. (Note: there were these weird windows with vertical venetian blinds behind us, which our backs brushed up against, occasionally). "Maybe you can go sit in a seat or something." (Translation: Go get your cynical, non-child-sponsoring [expletives] into a seat. Pronto.)

Building 429 played two songs and then we left. They entered the venue to the opening strains of "Where the Streets Have No Name" by U2, which I thought was odd, but somehow completely appropriate. Odd because it felt incongruous for one band to walk into the venue to a

---

[16] Who is actually 24 years old.

different band's music (sort of like Mike Tyson walking into the ring wearing a "Larry Holmes" robe), but completely appropriate because the whole evening felt like an exercise in people portraying what they thought other rock stars looked/sounded/thought like. In a nutshell, it feels like everybody is trying to be Bono right now inasmuch as Bono has become the poster child for rockers with a conscience who are trying to quote/unquote Change the World. However, sometimes I just want my rockers to rock.

I should add here that Building 429 has a song, called "Glory Defined," that I really like. The best way to describe it is that it's sort of like Arena Rock for Christians. Lots of heavy guitar riffs and a soaring/inspiring chorus. It's the kind of song that makes you want to do something great (like, apparently, sponsoring some little impoverished children).

I like Roy. He tells his story on a documentary called *Re-Generated: The Jason Roy Story*. The product of a broken home, with a drug-abusing father, Roy was assaulted and beaten severely on a basketball court in college. That moment, he says, was the impetus that propelled him into music.

I want to root for guys like this—guys who didn't have a pair of rich evangelical parents financing their pilgrimage to Nashville in search of rock and roll gold. In fact, Roy was kicked out of the house for refusing to quit his band to focus on school. It was only after winning a Dove Award that Roy felt like he began to re-gain the respect of his parents. His music, he says, even began to change his estranged father.

290 · A Hard Thing on a Beautiful Day

"He's our biggest fan," says Roy, emotionally. "He knows every lyric to every song, and sometimes when I'm having a bad day I'll call him up and he'll quote me the lyrics to my own songs to try to encourage me." It's hard not to root for this, and I do root for Jason Roy and Building 429.

My dilemma, of course, is that Jason Roy will go home to his tour bus feeling amazing tonight, because he changed the lives of twenty or so World Vision children who now have sponsors. And this may be completely justified, because it may be how God chose to work in the lives of those children, even though it felt crass and heavy-handed and weird to me. I, on the other hand, will go home feeling like a jerk for writing most of what I've written above.

One of my favorite pastors/writers, Dr. Martyn Lloyd-Jones, always said something to the effect that "You can't go for the heart, in evangelism; you have to go for the mind." There was nothing mind-oriented about what happened tonight—it was all church-camp-style emotional appeals. I felt like we were going to walk out *en masse* to roast marshmallows and then throw our pinecones (representing sin) into the fire. That being said, not every Christian event has to be a conference for seminary students, intellectuals[17], and PhD candidates. I guess I was looking for that balance between faith and works—and left feeling like many of those involved in Winter Blast were more excited about what they were doing for God, than what God

---

[17] Like Calvin College's "Festival of Faith and Music" which packages itself as "thoughtful" but still manages to come off as weird/obnoxious but in a completely different but no less self-congratulatory way.

had done for them.

They sounded good, I guess, inasmuch as sounding good involves playing your instruments well and looking like rock stars. And I guess that's what was weird about it. The whole show felt like people impersonating rock stars more than actual rock stars themselves. They played a song that I recognized, about which I got really excited, until Zach informed me that it was a song by a different band (The Newsboys). I'm so confused.

Maybe I'm overthinking all of this.

ABOUT THE AUTHOR

Ted Kluck is a professor, screenwriter, and award-winning author. He has written dozens of books, including *Why We're Not Emergent*, *Hello I Love You*, and *Facing Tyson*. His columns have run in *ESPN the Magazine*, *Sports Spectrum*, *The Jackson Sun*, and *USA Today*.

In 2010, Ted co-founded Gut Check Press and in 2014 was a founding member of both The Happy Rant Podcast and The Gut Check Podcast, both of which he continues to host. His first feature film, *Silverdome*, is currently in postproduction.

Ted has played professional indoor football, coached high school and college football, trained as a professional wrestler, served as a missionary overseas, and taught writing at several colleges and university. He holds an MFA from Ashland University and currently teaches journalism at Union University.

He lives in Humboldt, Tennessee with his lady and their two sons.

Made in the USA
Columbia, SC
18 September 2019